W 38

The Occult Experience

The Occult Experience

NEVILL DRURY

ROBERT HALE · LONDON

© Nevill & Susan Drury Publishing Pty Ltd, 1985
First published in Great Britain 1987

Robert Hale Ltd
Clerkenwell House
Clerkenwell Green
London EC1R 0HT

British Library Cataloguing in Publication Data

Drury, Nevill
   The occult experience.
   1. Psychical research
   I. Title
   133   BF1031

   ISBN 0-7090-2961-6

Printed in Great Britain by St Edmundsbury Press Ltd
Bound by WBC Bookbinders Ltd

Contents

Illustrations

Picture Credits
Walter Glover: 2, 5, 7; Jim Alan and Selena Fox: 19, 20; Marguerita Moore: 21. Other illustrations are from the author's collection.

Foreword

Nevill Drury's survey of key aspects of the occult and neo-pagan movement in Britain, Ireland, the USA, and Australia – the survey which produced his film, and in turn this book – is not only the adventure he admits it to have been. It is also a useful contribution to the understanding of our times.

Most people are aware that the occult seems currently fashionable; that mentioning astrological birth-signs, auras, or clairvoyance is acceptably trendy; that Tarot readers are to be found in every town; that feminists are challenging the accepted view of God as male; that alternative medicine is booming; and so on and so on. And probably most people suppose that these are passing phenomena, which will fade like so many others when they lose their novelty.

They are not, and they will not. Some of these symptoms may be mere ripples – but they are ripples on the surface of a significant rising tide.

We are at the end of an epoch, or rather of several interconnected epochs. The epoch of patriarchy, which has dominated us for roughly two millennia. The epoch of mechanical materialism, which dominated the scientific explosion of the past century or two and is now cracking at the seams, even among scientists. The epoch of watertight cultural compartments, now rapidly disintegrating in the face of instant worldwide communication. The epoch of rigid frontiers, on which Chernobyl is comment enough. The epoch of the work ethic, increasingly a sick joke as automation and the micro-chip abolish routine jobs which will never be revived. The epoch of unthinking exploitation of the environment . . . The list could of course be extended.

Increasing numbers are finding (either instinctively or by conscious analysis) that existing conventions — religious, philosophical, social, political, ethical — no longer meet the needs of such a fundamental period of change. And this is becoming more obvious as the rate of change itself accelerates almost daily.

Mere abandonment of established conventions does not solve the problem, except perhaps for the dedicated hermit. Something must take their place.

It is the search for that something which has triggered off the occult and neo-pagan explosion. Occultism, with its acceptance of multi-level reality, and its emphasis on development of the whole individual, appeals to many. Paganism, with its emphasis on respect for Mother Earth and its rejection of dogmatic stereotypes, offers an alternative to the authoritarianism and hypocrisy of so much of establishment religion (shortcomings which, incidentally, increasingly disturb many of its sincere believers).

Occultism and paganism, of course, overlap, and cannot always be separated. My wife Janet and I, for example, as practising witches, regard ourselves as both occultists and pagans; and so do the followers of many other paths within the spectrum.

Which of the paths one follows, if one feels in tune with the general approach, is an individual matter; and most occultists and pagans would agree that no one path is the 'only truth'. The concept of orthodoxy and heresy is alien to them. (Which does not prevent them, of course, from condemning attitudes which they regard as negative or 'black'; most of them, for example, would so brand Satanism.)

Accepting, as I think one must, that the occult and pagan explosion is a real and growing factor, one can study it by reading, or contacting, its various exponents. But it is helpful to start with an overall view of the field — and this is the value of Nevill's book, and the reason why we were so willing and honoured to be a part of his 'adventure'.

He is to be congratulated on making such a vividly representative selection of bodies and individuals, from Goddess-worshippers to artists, from witches to psychologists — and even some outspoken opponents of the movement; and on encouraging all of them to speak and act for themselves.

Stewart Farrar

Acknowledgements

Thanks are due to all of the occultists, witches, scientists and assorted visionaries who consented to be interviewed and who appear both in our film and in this book. My appreciation also to Frank Heimans and Martin Cohen of Cinetel Productions, Sydney, for the majority of the photographic illustrations used here, and to the film team — Geoffrey Simpson, Wolfgang Knochell, Kevin Kearney, Roy Mason and Cary Hamlyn, who made the documentary a reality.

Preface

Writing this book, and making the documentary film upon which it is based, have been very much an adventure for me. Between October 1984 when film director, Frank Heimans, and I first began meeting the mystics and occultists whom we wished to interview, through to March 1985 when the filming concluded, we were privileged to enter the lives of a wonderful range of people. We met shamans, witches, goddess-worshippers, visionary artists, psychologists, anthropologists, theologians and garden attendants. We talked with Kabbalists, ceremonial magicians, and practitioners of Voodoo and Egyptian magic. We experienced the occult *from the inside*.

This book is an overview of what happened on our journey and an account of the occult philosophies which were expressed. For some the occult was a path to power, for others a quest for spiritual enlightenment. Some were drawn by a close bond to Nature, to the sacred earth. Others were primarily exploring the rich tapestry of mythic symbols buried deep in the mind, or learning techniques for inducing altered states of consciousness. But all, we felt, were sincere in their beliefs, whether we agreed with them or not. And this, I hope, is the value of *The Occult Experience*. For here is a description of what occultists themselves believe — expressed, as far as possible, in the way it was told to us.

I feel like I am the earth, I'm sea,
I'm everything feminine.
And the priest and priestesses before me —
as I look into their eyes, and they look
into my eyes, there is a most incredible
openness that one doesn't find in the
mundane world.
We can only experience that within
the sacredness of a ritual . . .

LEVANAH

INTRODUCTION
Approaching the Occult

For those unfamiliar with occult beliefs, the world of magic and mysticism produces a/wide variety of responses. It can seem — to different people — frightening, potentially demonic or distinctly irrational. To some it seems outmoded or irrelevant, indeed for many the occult has little apparent value at all. The subject has attracted much shallow and sensational media coverage, with its more superficial aspects such as fortune telling, Sunday newspaper horoscopes and the belief in omens and portents, receiving the most public attention.

However, in recent times, there has been increasing interest in alternative belief systems, and although the term 'pagan' is still very much a coloured word, the core of these emerging beliefs has tended to lie outside the Judaeo-Christian tradition. Sometimes what we can call the new paganism — or neopaganism — surfaces in surprising ways, even in domains not considered religious by most.

Many people accept, for example, that meditation is ideal for treating stress-related forms of illness, and yet most of the available meditation techniques derive from non-Christian religions, especially Hinduism and Buddhism. There is also broad-based public support for alternative medicine and some of the major therapies are regarded as acceptable adjuncts to modern, orthodox treatment. Yet such approaches as these usually have a distinctly metaphysical base. Acupuncture theory for example, is based on the traditional Chinese concept of the flow of *yin* and *yang*. And while some acupuncturists now interpret the technique as a way of stimulating an endorphin (pain-killing) response from the brain, there is no doubt that most Chinese practitioners still find the metaphysical explanation more complete.

The other major healing tradition which has widespread public acceptance is hypnosis. Although it is now being applied in a clinical setting, the origins of hypnosis are found in Anton Mesmer's eighteenth-century theories of 'animal magnetism', and even earlier ideas which derive from the works of Paracelsus and the alchemists. Mesmer believed he could transfer a magnetic fluid or energy to his patients, and although modern hypnotherapists now consider it is more a case of stimulating the healing potential from within, the overriding belief is in the power to cause self-transformation — an essentially occult idea.

It may come as something of a surprise that the belief systems underlying acupuncture and hypnosis are remarkably similar to what we are calling here the neopagan viewpoint. In the first case a person is said to become well when the energies of the body are attuned to the *yin* and *yang* flow of the universe — in other words, we should attune ourselves to our external environment rather than fight against it. As we will see later in this book, one of the most profound reasons for the rise in pagan thought is an extension of the environmental perspective — the idea of reconnecting with the sacred earth — and there is now a commonly expressed 'alternative' belief in the possibility of 'healing the planet'. To this extent, then, there is a convergence of opinion from ostensibly unrelated areas of the social spectrum.

In the second instance, the evolution of mesmerism into hypnotherapy has a specific parallel in magical belief. The superstitious still believe it is possible to place spells on people, to transfer some sort of magical energy — malignant or enrapturing — to another person at a distance. However, most intelligent occultists have long since rejected this viewpoint and look instead within themselves for the healing powers of growth and self-transformation. Real magic then becomes simply a way of tapping into the inner potential and enhancing one's sensitivity to the many different facets of existence. The real miracles, to this extent, lie within us — a concept which gains support from the analysts and psychotherapists working within the Human Potential movement today.

The pagan perspective also shows itself in other ways. Massage and Tai Chi have taught us to respect our bodies rather than deny them and, in the latter case, that human expression through creative movement can be a sacred act. Not surprisingly, practitioners of modern witchcraft say much the same thing. They often perform their rituals naked because they feel this eliminates pretence and presents each person as they *really are* — and not how they would wish to appear. And in ceremonial invocations — in calls to the gods and spirits — there is, accordingly, the implicit belief that man and woman can themselves become sacred, lifting their ordinary lives, as it were, to a new octave: a more refined level of perception.

In all this, then, there is a belief that we have within

ourselves the potential for our own growth and renewal. Transcendental meditation says this, Zen Buddhism says this, and the western occult tradition says it also. But where the neopagan viewpoint has its most hostile reception is in a quite different quarter — from those highly structured and innately authoritarian religious organizations who believe that the truth is somehow fixed, tangible and dogmatic: that divine revelation can only descend to the people through a specific channel of command. It is to these people, especially fundamentalist Christians or dogmatic adherents aligned with any one specific creed, that the occult perspective presents the greatest challenge. And, accordingly, it is these people who are most inclined to condemn the occult as demonic and evil — a characteristically rigid response to an alternative belief system.

There is no doubt that the rise of rational and scientific thought has challenged the divine-authority base of mainstream Christianity to the extent that church attendance in modern times is now very much on the decline. So where does this leave the occult, and how do practitioners of magic and witchcraft respond to the modern world?

Ironically, the majority of occultists today are supporters of technology that is helpful to the community, and a surprisingly high number work as computer programmers, or in other related areas of industry. However, they believe that the demands of the urban existence should be complemented by being attuned to the broader world outside — a recognition that the cycles of Nature and the Universe as a whole provide a wider scope for meaning than the constrictions of office routine or adherence to a contrived work ethic. So in western society — in Britain, in the United States, and in Australia — the pagans work in offices, commute, and live ordinary suburban lives. However they also believe that the occult, in its most positive sense, provides an extra dimension which is valuable to the quality of their existence on this planet.

The Christian response to occult belief has varied in different western countries and appears to be directly related to the degree of liberal thought found in different religious institutions. In Britain, the Churches' Fellowship for Psychical and Spiritual Studies was founded in 1954, on an interdenominational basis, to explore the possibility that the study of parapsychology and mysticism might throw light on Christ's miracles and other aspects of the faith. Its patrons have included several leading English clerics, among them Canon Pearce-Higgins, the Reverend Dr Leslie Weatherhead and the Reverend Lord Soper, as well as the distinguished Australian-born physicist, Dr Raynor Johnson, and the philosopher, Sir George Trevelyan.

In Australia, however, the official Church response has been more guarded. In 1974 the Anglican Archbishop of Sydney, Marcus Loane, agreed to the establishment of a Commission of Enquiry into the occult — only the second such enquiry in a Protestant country since the Middle Ages.[1] A board of investigators was duly assembled — including several prominent theologians, two academics and a psychiatrist, and the Report of the Commission was released in 1975. According to the authors of the report, the occult was potentially Satanic and linked to decadent tendencies in modern society. In particular, it was claimed that 'occultism may provide pornography with a religious base to work from'. There was concern at the widespread incidence of belief in astrology, Tarot cards and spiritualism, and the Commission advocated protective legislation to prevent children from being exposed to ouija boards and other occult paraphernalia.

Media responses to the Anglican Commission enquiry: 'The occult is dangerous'

Ten years later, Dean Shilton — a member of the Anglican Commission — still holds substantially to the fundamentals of that position:

'The Church does regard the occult as dangerous . . . because it can lead people into all kinds of difficulties,' says Shilton. But he does not deny the existence of the supernatural — indeed he believes it to be central to the Christian viewpoint. The occult itself, though, is potentially in league with the Devil, who is himself a supernatural being with a real and tangible existence.

On the related subject of demonic possession Dean Shilton says the Anglican Church is now less inclined to advocate exorcism than it used to, although this seemed to be the best solution in 1974. Exorcism within the mainstream churches has in fact diminished since the time of the Anglican Commission, and a leading church advocate of exorcism at that time, the Reverend Peter Hobson, is no longer active. Making the point that many cases of demon possession can be simply explained as schizophrenia Shilton notes:

'Before we can say that a person is possessed by a devil you have to look at the medical and psychological side first.' He is, however, aware that Christian exorcism is still prevalent, especially among the Pentecostal and fundamentalist devotees. But 'exorcism' is no longer the favoured word. Pentecostalists now refer to their rites of exorcism as 'Christian deliverance ministry' and there are many sincere devotees and laypeople who believe they can cast out spirits of evil.

Ruth and Garry Penhall conduct deliverance sessions in their spacious double-storey home in Burwood, a suburb of Sydney. Ruth came to Christian deliverance by way of palmistry — a practice she now considers evil and pernicious — and her husband is a born-again fundamentalist Christian with a

'The range of possessing spirits is potentially endless' (from a drawing by Rosaleen Norton)

passion for driving out spirits of possession. For the Penhalls, the range of possessing spirits is potentially endless, and includes devils of self-pity, loneliness, torment, insomnia, seduction, despair, homosexuality, superstition and idolatry, among others. The Penhalls believe that spirits like to dwell in a 'watery' environment — especially the human body, which is substantially fluid — and the act of exorcism therefore calls for the spirits to depart 'to dry places' — where they will linger until being cast into a lake of fire and brimstone after Christ's return to earth. The Penhalls have also delivered believers from the 'deceptive spirits' of Buddhism, Hare Krishna-style Hinduism, Islam, witchcraft, yoga and meditation — as well as from 'devils of error' lurking within Christianity itself. Demons, they say, are waiting all around us ready to pounce, and very few people indeed are able to purge themselves completely of their influence.

Those requiring deliverance arrange to be interviewed by the Penhalls and then come to their home at an allotted time. Here they lie on a soft carpet and are prayed for by a small group. The exorcism then begins with a fervent appeal for the spirits to depart in the name of Jesus. This might include such commands as: 'Fear of suicide, I renounce you; fear of death I renounce you...I break the generation of spirits...go forth now, go forth to dry places...'

Sessions sometimes last for several hours and subjects frequently writhe on the floor in trance as they wrestle with the departing spirits.

'People come to us,' says Garry Penhall, 'and they're not even aware that they have demons in them. They're suffering from various kinds of hurts and problems and, since the ministry of Jesus included the casting out of demons, that's what we do — as His ambassadors.'

Ruth is adamant that the occult attracts a wide range of devils: 'Occult demons are very prevalent because many people go to palm readers, or they have their Tarot cards read, or they go to spiritualist churches, or worship foreign gods. Because these people don't worship the One True God they are not protected from the onslaught of demons and spirits that come in to torment them.'

This is unquestionably an extreme viewpoint — even

within the Christian Church. While the Penhalls categorize Buddhism, Hinduism, Taoism, Islam, Bahai'ism, Theosophy, Freemasonry and Occultism as 'false religions', Dean Shilton is less dogmatic on this score. Occult beliefs, he says, may be inferior to the Christian perspective but they nevertheless belong somewhere on a religious spectrum:

'I think there *is* a spiritual dimension in the pagan approach because I believe we all have a soul or spirit and this seeks to express itself in some way. That can be in a variety of forms — such as spiritism, animism, Buddhism, Islam — or Christianity. At least the other religions give expression to a spiritual dimension...'

American theologian Dr Gordon Melton agrees. A former minister of Chicago's Emmaus United Methodist Church, Melton is one of the few Christian theologians and academics in the United States who have explored alternative belief systems in depth.[2] As author of *The Encyclopedia of American Religions* he is widely admired by the neopagan community for his tolerance and understanding. Melton met Donna Cole — one of the first practising witches in Chicago — in the early 1970s, and then began attending neopagan meetings in Minneapolis. Various articles of his were published in the now defunct occult journal *The Green Egg* and this, he says, legitimized him as an objective scholar of American paganism among the witches themselves. In 1979 he began collecting sociological material on occult beliefs and worked with the Pagan Council in Chicago, circulating a questionnaire to practising witches, occultists and goddess-worshippers. He also participated in magical ceremonies in order to experience them for himself. This hasn't led to his conversion, for Melton is still very much a Christian evangelist, but it was an opportunity to understand the appeal of occultism first-hand.

'I have the greatest respect for many of the pagans that I have met and worked with,' says Melton. 'I have found them very intelligent people, and I've found among their leaders people who were intuitive, mystical and spiritual...'

How does he feel about their non-Christian perspective?

'I would wish and hope that people could have found what they have found in paganism, in the Christian Church, but not having found it there I'm glad they have found it *somewhere*. They're tapping a mystical depth that is present in all humanity. It certainly *is* present in the Church, although it is not as visible as we'd like it to be.'

Melton believes it is the search for experience, rather than adherence to creed or dogma, which has led to the increasing interest in other religious traditions:

'Eastern and pagan religions both have a very real appeal on a spiritual level — the feeling of experiencing spiritual reality — and this draws people to these faiths. They experience something that, particularly in the older churches, we don't experience as much any more.'

His views on the Pentecostal revival are also interesting because, in contrast to the Penhalls, he finds substantial similarities between Christians who summon Jesus and the Holy Ghost and occultists who call on pagan deities in their ceremonies:

'Any religious group which is interested in a strongly felt emotional religion,' says Melton, 'tends to do the same thing in order to raise the power. If you look at right-wing Pentecostalism and at the pagan movement, you find that there is the same attempt to create sacred space and to have unusual phenomena happen. Among Pentecostalists it is speaking in tongues and healing. Among pagans it is "raising the cone of power" and working magic. But to an outsider they are

The traditional concept of witches as haggard crones — an illustration published in England in 1619

structurally very similar in what they are doing — even though the words and music and specific actions are quite different.'

Melton also emphasizes that for far too long Christians, and the public at large, have been confusing witches with Satanists — an unfortunate legacy from the persecution of witches during the medieval Inquisition.

'Modern pagans have got an uphill job to retrieve this image,' he says, 'but fortunately they *have* done that to a large extent. However the prejudice of the Church stands against them because the Church would like to have Satanists as their competitors, rather than pagans and goddess-worshippers. It's easier to fight them on that line.'

'Luckily,' he adds, 'inside the Church I've found a general

degree of acceptance for my research and my colleagues certainly pay attention to the information I bring them concerning various alternative religions. A few of my more conservative friends still get upset but overall they are very much a minority.'

At this point one may be drawn to ask: what exactly *are* the common themes in occult belief and what are the areas of dissimilarity? What exactly do witches do, and how do their philosophies and practices differ from those found in ceremonial magic, the Kabbalah, and other forms of mysticism?

As one would expect, the answer to these questions is not a simple one. The neopagan movement is now highly eclectic and widely dispersed, and no two groups function in an exactly similar way. There is a widespread variance of opinion over what constitutes true initiation and whether some sort of hierarchy is important or not. Some groups have both male and female membership whereas others restrict themselves exclusively to one sex or the other. Some function best with a charismatic leader whereas others are more egalitarian. And some groups are more open than others with regard to their ceremonies, invocations and beliefs.

Nevertheless, there are areas of common ground and it is possible to provide a broad overview of what witches and occultists believe. And while the groups and practitioners described in later chapters have their own distinctive identity, I believe that — in a very real way — they do represent the broad range of occult perspectives as we find them today. The occult — once a hidden tradition — is becoming more open, and the mysteries are now more accessible to the public than they have been for hundreds of years.

Witchcraft

Modern witchcraft is often referred to as Wicca from the Old English words *wicca* (masculine) and *wicce* (feminine) meaning 'a practitioner of witchcraft'. The word *wiccan*, meaning 'witches' occurs in the Laws of King Alfred (*circa* 890 AD) and the verb *wiccian* — 'to bewitch' — was also used in this context. Some witches believe the words connote a wise person, and Wicca is sometimes known as 'the Craft of the Wise'.

Witchcraft in essence is a Nature-based religion with the Great Goddess as its principal deity. She can take many forms, the Great Mother or Mother Nature, or more specifically Artemis, Astarte, Athene, Demeter, Diana, Aphrodite, Dana, Hathor, Isis or Persephone — among many others. The High Priestess of the coven incarnates the spirit of the Goddess in a ceremonial context when the High Priest 'draws down the Moon' into her body. In witchcraft, the High Priestess is the receptacle of wisdom and intuition and is symbolized by the Cup, whereas her consort is represented by the short sword or dagger. Many witchcraft rituals feature the act of uniting dagger and cup as a symbol of sexual union, and there is also a comparable relationship in Celtic mythology between the sacred oak tree and Mother Earth. Accordingly, the High Priest, or consort, is sometimes known as the Oak King — a reference to the revered Oak of the Celts — and at other times as Cernunnos: 'The Horned One'. In witchcraft the Horned God personifies fertility, and in ancient Greece the Great God Pan — the goat-footed god — was a symbol of Nature and the universal Life Force. There is no connection between the Horned God of witchcraft and the Christian horned Devil although, since the witchcraft persecutions of the Middle

Ages, this has been a common error.

Witchcraft covens vary in size although traditionally the membership number is thirteen — consisting of six men, six women and the High Priestess. When the group exceeds this number, some members leave to form a new coven. Witches take special magical names which they use in a ritual context, and they meet for their ceremonies at specific times of the year. These meetings, or sabbats, are related to the cycles of Nature and the harvesting of crops.

The four major sabbats are:

Candlemas (2 February) known by the Celts as *Imbolc*

May Eve (30 April), or *Beltane*

Lammas (1 August), or *Lughnassadh*

Halloween (31 October), or *Samhain*

In addition there are four minor sabbats — the two solstices at midsummer and midwinter, and the two equinoxes in spring and autumn.

In pre-Christian times, *Imbolc* was traditionally identified with the first signs of spring; *Beltane* was a fertility celebration when the sacred oak was burned, mistletoe cut, and sacrifices made to the gods; *Lughnassadh*, which was related to autumn and the harvesting of crops, celebrated both the gathering in of produce and the continuing fertility of the earth; and *Samhain* represented the transition from autumn to winter and was associated with bonfires to keep away the chilly winter winds. *Samhain* was also a time when the spirits of the dead could return to earth to be once again with their loves ones.

Modern witches still meet in their covens to celebrate these

Celtic rites although, in the southern hemisphere, most Wiccan practitioners adjust the sabbats to equate with the appropriate season. Sabbats are a time for fellowship, ceremonial and initiation, and after the rituals have been performed, there is feasting, drinking and merriment.

Witchcraft ceremonies take place in a magic circle which can either be inscribed on the floor of the temple, or marked in the earth at a special meeting place — for example, in a grove or on the top of a sacred hill. The earth is swept with a ritual broomstick for purification and the four elements are ascribed to the four directions: Earth in the north; Air in the east; Fire in the south; and Water in the west. The altar is traditionally placed in the north. Beings known as the 'Lords of the Watchtowers' are believed to govern the four quarters and are invoked in rituals for blessings and protection.

Within the circle and present on the altar are the witch's *Book of Shadows* (a book of rituals and invocations), a bowl of water, a dish of salt, candles, a symbolic scourge (representing will and determination), a bell, a cord to bind candidates in initiation, and consecrated symbols of the elements: a pentacle or disc (Earth/feminine); a cup (Water/feminine); a censer (Fire/masculine) and a wand (Air/masculine). The High Priestess has her own *athame*, or ritual dagger, and the sword of the High Priest rests on the ground before the altar.

Modern witchcraft recognizes three initiations. The first confers witch-status upon the neophyte, the second promotes a first-degree witch to the position of High Priestess or High Priest, and the third celebrates the bonding of High Priestess and High Priest in the Great Rite: either real or symbolic sexual union.[3]

There is also an emphasis in witchcraft on the three-fold aspect of the Great Goddess in her role as Maid (youth, enchantment), Mother (maturity, fulfilment), and Crone (old age, wisdom). This symbolic personification of the phases of womanhood as represented by, for example, the Celtic triad, Brigid-Dana-Morrigan, and the Greek goddess in her three aspects, Persephone-Demeter-Hecate, or the three Furies, Alecto (goddess of beginnings) — Tisiphone (goddess of continuation) — Megaera (goddess of death and rebirth), is particularly emphasized. by several of the feminist Wicca groups in their development of 'women's mysteries'. As American neopagan Z Budapest writes in her *Holy Book of Women's Mysteries* (Part Two): 'Images of the Mother Goddess, female principle of the universe and source of all life, abound... [for she is the] goddess of ten thousand names.'

On a practical level Wiccan ceremonies can involve spells of enchantment, invocations for healing, and initiations which lead a coven member from one grade of advancement to the next. Witches also conduct their own type of weddings known as 'handfastings', binding Wiccans for a specified time ranging from a year and a day to 'eternity', and also 'wiccanings', the pagan counterpart of christenings. Coven members tend to become close friends and the group functions rather like a family, with the High Priestess and High Priest taking a caring, parental role for other members of the coven.

White Magic

Magic is usually classified as 'black' or 'white', and this has very much to do with intent. Black magic is pursued in order to cause harm to another person — through injury, illness or misfortune — and it also aims to enhance the personal power of the magician in bringing about this result. White magic, on the other hand, has a beneficial outcome and is often associated with rites of healing, with eliminating evil or disease, and with the expansion of consciousness.

From an occult point of view the power of positive thinking, which underlies many self-help philosophies, is simply white magic. So too are all forms of faith-healing and the religious act of praying to God for a positive outcome in cases of illness and misfortune. So it is white magic which is of the most interest to us in the context of the modern occult revival.

The tradition of western ceremonial magic overlaps with Wicca but is by no means the same. Ritual magicians do not refer to the Lords of the Watchtowers but instead invoke and visualize the four archangels of Judaism, and they use Hebrew god-names like Adonai, Shaddai and Elohim. Their orientation also tends to be patriarchal rather than feminist.

Most ceremonial occultists today have been strongly influenced by the techniques and philosophy of the Hermetic Order of the Golden Dawn, a late nineteenth-century magical society described in the next chapter. This style of occultism did not focus primarily on the worship of the Goddess as modern witchcraft does, but on the idea of personal spiritual transformation or rebirth. The initial aim of the white magician is to find the healing god within — an idea rather similar to Carl Jung's concept of 'individuation' or inner wholeness. This can entail contacting both male or female energies in the psyche although in the Golden Dawn, which tended to focus on male rebirth deities, the focus was solar and male, rather than lunar or female.

Occultists use ceremonial to stimulate their imaginations, to help them enter a state of enlarged awareness, which is almost like participating in the myths and legends of a forgotten time. But these mythic symbols represent processes of self-fulfilment, so images like the Holy Grail (which is the Ace of Cups in the Tarot) become a motif for spiritual inspiration and enlightenment, and resurrected gods like Osiris, Jesus and Christian Rosenkreutz represent the death of one's old life and the rebirth of the new.

White magic is 'occult' or hidden, simply because many of its teachings and ideas were deemed heretical by the medieval Christian Church and so practitioners had to go underground. In the early Christian centuries the Gnostic sects advocated the mystical idea of releasing the soul from its bondage in the body and practised techniques for elevating human consciousness to purer, more transcendent levels of awareness. This concept was viewed with suspicion by Church leaders like Irenaeus and Tertullian, because it eroded the hierarchical idea that divine inspiration could only be received through one official channel — that provided by the Church. In the Middle Ages all visionary movements such as the Cathars, the Albigenses, the Bogomils, and later the pantheists, Freemasons, Rosicrucians and Kabbalists, were clearly suspect in the eyes of the authorities and subject to the most intense persecution. This is an intrinsic problem with all forms of mysticism which compete with a religious organization that depends for its power base on well-defined patterns of belief.

The distinguished psychologist, Professor Charles Tart, says:

'My researches have shown me that the most important spiritual and religious ideas and visions have come about in altered states of consciousness, and as a matter of fact you have to be in an altered state of consciousness to fully appreciate them. The tragedy of ordinary religion is that people in an ordinary state of consciousness try to grasp certain ideas and principles that aren't graspable in ordinary consciousness, and then it's no wonder that religion seems shallow and illogical.'

Practitioners of white magic and mysticism believe that it is through their rituals, their trance states, through invocations, prayer and song — and the altered states they produce — that the most profound areas of consciousness can be tapped. But this hardly endears them to religious orthodoxy. While many occultists believe that their practices complement mainstream religion, and simply provide it with more depth and mystery, such an approach is bound to be viewed with suspicion. As Professor Tart comments further:

'Both our culture and our religious institutions are very suspicious of altered states of consciousness. Religions, which were so important in the formation of culture, all started with people having experiences in altered states. But they became secular institutions and got tied in with establishments. You then get a fear that if someone has any new revelations they might not match the new doctrines. And so religion ends up often conspiring to keep people from having genuine religious experiences.'

White magic draws on esoteric spiritual traditions which do provide religious experiences, for this is precisely what true occult initiation is all about. The form of the initiation itself, however, can vary considerably. It may be that the devotee identifies with Osiris, and feels within himself a new mystical awakening, of looking at life in a renewed and revitalized way. Or it may be more a mystical journey through the planes of consciousness described in such systems as the Jewish Kabbalah, with its complex symbol of the Tree of Life.

Eventually though, as English Kabbalist and scholar Warren Kenton (Z'ev ben Shimon Halevi) points out, all authentic mystical and magical beliefs are heading for the same place:

'If one looks at all the great religions — and my definition of a great religion is one that contains all the possibilities open to man in his relationship to the universe and to God — you will always find an esoteric core. Now, that esoteric core must ultimately go back to the Holy One and to the way the universe is constructed and how a human being is composed. You must inevitably go beyond the realm of culture and form. The Chinese, the Arab, the Red Indian, the Jew, the Christian, must all reach a point where they pass in this work beyond race and beyond culture, and they must meet as human beings — because, after all, they are all the image of God. How else could it be?'

Like Professor Tart, Kenton emphasizes the visionary origins of religion and the difficulty this poses for the orthodox Church:

'One has the problem of a polarity between the external religion — be it Church or Synagogue — and the internal part of religion. I think one has to remember that all religions start with a mystical experience, be it Moses or Abraham or Mohammed or Buddha. And those great ones were mystics. The manifestation of their teaching, however, in coming down to the level of ordinary life, has to take up various forms. It has to take up a structure, rituals, practices, ethics and so forth. And so one can say that the outer part of religion will always look at the interior part a little apprehensively because it is performing *the role.* And very often you get the role without the content. The great periods of religious history are when both the inner and the outer are working as one.'

It is clear, nevertheless, that magic and mysticism — like religious teachings of all kinds — present themselves on various levels. Many people are drawn to the occult as a path of power, as a way of dominating lower-ranking members in the hierarchy or in asserting a grandiose role for themselves as head of a sacred tradition. These, says Kenton, are the human failings, the limitations which people place on themselves in their quest for higher vision. Kenton finds it useful to distinguish between 'high' magic and 'low' magic, and he relates this to the Kabbalah itself — a mystical tradition which has provided western magic with much of its spiritual and esoteric content.

'Kabbalah is basically concerned with coming to know God and to serve God. In fact, one of its names is the "work of Unification", or "the work of Creation", in which one works in conjunction with the Holy One to bring about self-realization — not only of oneself but the whole of mankind. In the case of occultism this may also be the case, but you can divide occultism — like magic — into high and low. There are people who wish to know about hidden things — which is what occultism means — and those who simply want to know about the hidden worlds to make use of them for personal reasons. This is the difference between high magic and low magic. Somebody practising high magic would be on a parallel to the Sufis, the Kabbalists and the Christian mystics, while those drawn to low magic would be people who use a little knowledge in order to accomplish certain things for personal ends.'

In fact, says Kenton, this distinction applies to all forms of religious expression. In both mainstream religions and the occult traditions alike there are always people who are attracted for selfish reasons. 'They wish,' he says, 'to become men and women of power, or to manipulate people. Those who enter any spiritual tradition for a higher reason have a completely different outlook. They are not interested in power and their hallmark is precisely that quality. That's how you differentiate between the high and low in any spiritual tradition... every true religion is ultimately the same.'

White magic, from this perspective, then becomes a journey of consciousness from the lower and more restricted aspects of mind to the more profound and universal aspects of human consciousness. For it is through self-realization that the mystical theme of a sacred unity with the universe, and ultimately with all other sentient beings, reveals itself. As occult history shows, however, the goal is not easily achieved. The world of magic and mysticism, as many critics have correctly observed, is littered with tales and incidents of misused power and self-glorification, of charlatanism and deceit. Sometimes, it would seem, the quest for transcendence is simply too great, and the human factor — once again — asserts its presence.

This human factor is obviously present in the occult today. In their most positive aspects, magic and witchcraft present a profound bond with Nature, a link with the cycles and rhythms of existence, and with the beneficial and inspiring aspects of human self-expression. But the negative aspects of misplaced power, of selfishness and of self-glorification are there too, and must be placed in perspective. Despite these shortcomings, however, the occult presents a fascinating journey within the world of human potential. With this in mind we have chosen to present the full spectrum of occult belief, from what seems good to what seems possibly evil, from what exalts light to that which draws on the powers of darkness. This book, like the film on which it is based, is presented in a non-judgemental way. Like Warren Kenton, I believe that there are many paths to the same place and it is the sheer diversity of human expression which makes the world of the occult as rich and colourful as it is today.

One thing is certain: the old gods are stirring from their slumber yet again and reaffirming their hold on our imagination. The occult, in both its folly and its wisdom, leads us back to their domain.

1. The first enquiry into exorcism began in 1963 when the Bishop of Exeter in England appointed a joint Anglican–Roman Catholic investigation of this phenomenon.

2. Since the time of his interview Dr Melton has transferred to the University of California at Santa Barbara.

3. For full descriptions of these initiations see Janet and Stewart Farrar, *The Witches' Way*, London 1984.

CHAPTER 1
Pathways into Magic

On the first day of December, 1947, the famous occultist and ceremonial magician, Aleister Crowley, died in the English beach resort town of Hastings. For those who had admired him it was the end of an era. In his time he had earned both praise and notoriety, not only as an exotic ritualist but as a prolific writer, explorer, self-publicist and womanizer. He had synthesized techniques of western magic, yoga and ancient Egyptian religion, he had conducted occult ceremonies in the Algerian desert, he had declared himself to be 'The Great Beast' — successor to Jesus and Mohammed — and he had been evicted from his 'sex abbey' in Sicily by Mussolini in 1923. Much of his subsequent career had then been spent in pursuit of the elusive Whore Of Babalon, and his string of mistresses seemed endless. Indeed, in his own way, he had become a legend in his lifetime.

Crowley's detractors maintain that he gave the western occult tradition the bad name which it has never quite dispelled, and there is some truth in this. However Crowley's influence certainly did not diminish with his death, and during the 1960s — when there was a type of occult revival — there was once again renewed interest in his writings, and most of his books were subsequently reissued. Even more significant, though, was the impact he had on Gerald Gardner, one of the founders of modern witchcraft and, in his own right, a seminal influence on contemporary neopagan thought. And it is ironic that the other leading figure in the 1960s witchcraft revival, Alex Sanders, now lives in quiet and inconspicuous retirement in Bexhill-on-Sea, just a few kilometres along the road from Crowley's last resting place.

Aleister Crowley undoubtedly brought western magic to public attention, especially through his more lurid writings like *Diary of a Drug Fiend*, which was described in the *Sunday Express* of 26 November 1922 as 'a book for burning'. But there was substantially more depth to the occult tradition than this, as his critics would have discovered had they investigated the magical group that had trained him — the Hermetic Order of the Golden Dawn. For, as Crowley discovered when he joined, here was an occult organization that not only drew on far-ranging mythic and esoteric traditions but also provided, through its ceremonial structures and practices, a framework for modern magical belief.

In 1887 a London coroner named Dr Wynn Westcott obtained a manuscript written in cipher from a deceased estate. It included five Masonic rituals and had belonged to a member of an English Rosicrucian group. Westcott saw in the material the potential for developing a new occult order and he invited his friend, Samuel Mathers, to expand the rituals into a new system — one which would encompass all the major elements of the western mystery tradition. And it would not be out of place, thought Westcott, to claim for the new order an ancient lineage, thereby establishing its clear credentials as part of the hidden wisdom of the West.

Aleister Crowley — master magician

As is well known to occult historians, Westcott then announced that he had found among the papers of the cipher manuscript the name and address of a certain Fraulein Anna Sprengel — an eminent Rosicrucian adept. He was thus able to maintain, in announcing his discovery to the Theosophists and Freemasons of the day, that he had found a link between English Rosicrucianism and its earlier German counterpart. The latter, after all, traced its inspirational source to the mysteries of Christian Rosenkreutz, described in three publications issued in Germany around 1614, and purporting to derive from an ancient occult brotherhood. One of these books, *Fama Fraternitas*, described Christian Rosenkreutz's meeting with the Wise Men of Damcar; another, called *Chymische Hochziet Christiani Rosenkreutz*, gave details of a symbolic marriage and 'secret books of wisdom', while the third, *Confession Fraternitas R. C.*, invited members of the public to join the order.

There was a clear precedent here for Westcott to emulate the example of the German Rosicrucians, and Mathers was able to rise to the occasion. The ceremonial rituals he formulated were quite brilliant in their conception and have remained influential among practising occultists to this day.

Mathers chose as his core framework the Kabbalistic Tree of Life, which describes ten spheres of consciousness, or *sephiroth*, between man and godhead. Simply expressed, the first four *sephiroth* represent, respectively, the world of waking consciousness (*Malkuth*), the sphere of sexuality and fertility (*Yesod*), the rational intellect (*Hod*) and love and the emotions (*Netzach*). Mathers' rituals were intended to stimulate these spheres of consciousness and provide a solid grounding for the Golden Dawn teachings themselves. This in turn would lead to the experience of spiritual rebirth in

Tiphareth, at the very centre of the Tree of Life.

The Tiphareth ritual of Adeptus Minor evoked the imagery of the Christian Rosenkreutz legend and also linked the figure of Jesus Christ with the Egyptian god Osiris, as parallel examples of resurrected gods. The candidate had to undergo a symbolic burial in the Tomb of the Adepti and emerge from it as one spiritually renewed: 'I am the First and the Last. I am He that liveth and was dead...I am the purified. I have passed through the Gates of Darkness into Light.'

Beyond Tiphareth were further mysteries, revealed in an inner order known by a different name: the Rosae Rubae et Aurea Crucis (the Red Rose and Cross of Gold). This encompassed those transcendent spheres of consciousness between Tiphareth and the Trinity, and knowledge of these spiritual realities was restricted to Golden Dawn initiates.

Mathers and Westcott meanwhile assumed ritual grades that placed themselves at the head of the second order — a convenient position located just below God, Creator of the Universe.

This was a regrettable move, however well intentioned it may have been at the time. The problem of spiritual hierarchy has been an ongoing one in all occult groups for it invariably leads to despotism, power factions and the debasement of spiritual intent. Unfortunately the Golden Dawn proved vulnerable to these all too human tendencies and declined, around 1918, into a number of schisms and splinter groups. However, in its early years it held much promise for it drew into its ranks some of the leading mystical thinkers of the day.

Arthur Edward Waite, the distinguished Kabbalistic and Hermetic scholar, became a member, and so too did William Butler Yeats — later a Nobel Prize winner for literature. The fantasy writers Arthur Machen and Algernon Blackwood both joined, and so also did Allan Bennett — an influential English occultist who later became Bhikku Ananda Metteya and helped found the British Buddhist Society. Other members included Gerald Kelly, later President of the Royal Academy, the noted actresses Annie Horniman and Florence Farr, the Scottish lawyer Dr John Brodie-Innes and Maud Gonne — later a major figure in the Irish Nationalist movement.

Aleister Crowley was introduced to the Golden Dawn by Allan Bennett and initiated as a neophyte on 18 November 1898. He quickly rose through the ceremonial grades and not only ascended through three ritual stages in two months but also undertook a lengthy six-month ritual attributed to the medieval magician Abramelin the Mage. This experience was important in his spiritual development for as his biographer John Symonds has written in *The Great Beast*:

'He stood within the Divine Light with a crown upon his head; the earth opened for him to enter into its very centre, where he climbed the peak of a high mountain. Many dragons sprang upon him as he approached the Secret Sanctuary but he overcame all with a word. This was an alchemical vision of his success in the Great Work. Crowley realized that he was born with all the talents required for a great magician.[1]

Mathers had now moved to Paris to translate esoteric texts and Yeats had become head of the Golden Dawn. Crowley tried to dislodge his Irish rival from this senior post but after failing in the endeavour went off, somewhat petulantly, on a series of international travels — through Mexico, the United States, Ceylon and India. Finally he arrived in Cairo, where he was to have a major magical revelation.

Here, on 14 March 1904, in a room near the Boulak Museum, Crowley performed a magical ceremony invoking

Thoth, the Egyptian god of Wisdom. His wife Rose, meanwhile, had become drowsy — as if entering a state of trance. She announced to her husband that Horus was 'waiting' for him in the Boulak Museum.

Inside, she and Crowley came upon a statue of Horus in the form of Ra-Hoor-Khuit, the risen god. Crowley was intrigued that the exhibit's listing was 666 — the number of the Great Beast in the *Book of Revelations.*

Crowley and his wife returned to the hotel and he now performed a ritual for Horus. Once again Rose fell into a state of trance and began to dictate a series of pronouncements purporting to come from a discarnate Egyptian entity called Aiwass. It was now proclaimed that a new magical epoch — the Aeon of Horus — had begun, with Crowley as its leader. Traditional ceremonial magic as practised in the Golden Dawn was henceforth superseded and replaced by a form of sexual magic. The new mystery teachings would focus instead on the creative bond between the gods and goddesses who had brought the universe into existence. Crowley himself would incarnate for the world the sexual union of Nuit and Hadit and in so doing would take the role of the chosen god-child.

Crowley now had no further use for the Golden Dawn and wrote to Samuel Mathers telling him that his system of magic was obsolete. Crowley's subsequent career would then lead him in 1909 to perform homosexual magical ceremonies in the Algerian desert with poet Victor Neuburg, and to establish an Abbey in Cefalu, Sicily, where the sexual mysteries could be practised in ceremonial form. Crowley named the establishment the Abbey of Thelema, after the Greek word meaning 'will'. He was now proclaiming his famous dictum: 'Do what thou wilt shall be the whole of the Law' and was well aware of the magical responsibility upon his shoulders. As

Aiwass had instructed him: 'Now ye shall know that the chosen priest and apostle of infinite space is the prince-priest, the Beast; and in his woman, called the Scarlet Woman, is all power given. They shall gather my children into their fold; they shall bring the glory of the stars into the hearts of men.'

At the Abbey Crowley had a new lover, Swiss-born American bohemian Leah Hirsig, but it was an affair that couldn't last, for his sexual relationships were invariably short-lived and Crowley tired quickly of his women. In later years there were several other 'scarlet women' in his life but these too, like images in the wind, would all prove ephemeral. By his own admission a truly satisfactory comrade in the mysteries of Nuit and Hadit was never found, and towards the end of his life Crowley confessed himself to be 'perplexed'.

However Crowley's escapades in sexual magic had not gone unnoticed and in 1946 two of his admirers, Arnold Crowther and Gerald Gardner, paid him a visit at Hastings. It was a significant meeting because Crowther and Gardner were both practitioners of modern witchcraft, and now Wicca and modern western magic were crossing paths — perhaps for the first time. Gardner and Crowley got on very well together and this led to further discussions between the two men until Crowley's death the following year.

Gardner had come to magic rather late in life. Born in 1884 at Blundellsands, near Liverpool, he came from a well-to-do family and was of Scottish descent. His father's family had managed the oldest private timber trade company in the British Empire and several of his ancestors had been mayors of Liverpool. These included Vice-Admiral Alan Gardner who was commander-in-chief of the channel fleet against Napoleon in 1807.

By 1936 Gerald Gardner was, himself, a man of independent means, having made a fortune as a rubber planter in Malaya. He was also interested in the history of Malayan civilizations and had written a book titled *Keris and Other Malay Weapons* — a pioneering study of the history and folklore of local armaments.

After his retirement Gardner and his wife settled in the New Forest area of Hampshire and, just prior to the outbreak of the Second World War, he made contact with a group of occultists in the area. Calling themselves the Fellowship of Crotona, they held theatrical performances which they claimed to be 'Rosicrucian' in character. However, some members of the Fellowship had links with a witchcraft coven and regular sabbat meetings were also being held at that time in the New Forest.

Gardner claimed that in 1939 he was initiated into witchcraft by 'Old Dorothy' Clutterbuck, a woman whose existence, until recently, had been subject to doubt. Doreen Valiente, an authority on witchcraft origins, has now been able to establish that 'Old Dorothy' was the daughter of Thomas St Quintin Clutterbuck, a captain of the 14th Sikhs, although the antiquity of her coven, of course, cannot be proven. 'Old Dorothy' herself was hardly the crone her name suggests. She was well-to-do and when she died in 1951 her estate was valued in excess of 60,000 pounds.

Gardner, meanwhile, described much of what he experienced in the coven in his novel *High Magic's Aid*, published in 1949. At that time the practice of witchcraft was still forbidden by law, and the activities described in the book had to be portrayed as fiction. Two years later, following a campaign by the British spiritualists, the Witchcraft Act was repealed and the Old Religion was allowed, at last, to come forth from the shadows. Gardner, for one, was pleased by this development for he believed witchcraft should be more open in its pursuits and appeal to a broader public.

During his meetings with Crowley, Gardner had shared many insights with his magical colleague and Crowley, in turn, made him an honorary member of his sexual magic order, the Ordo Templi Orientis. Repaying the tribute, Gardner began to use quotations from Crowley in his ceremonial rites and it is also likely that substantial sections of Gardner's magical credo was written by Crowley and then fused with a traditional *Book of Shadows.*

Other aspects of Gardnerian witchcraft, however, are quite likely his own invention. One of these is the modern tendency for witches to work naked, or 'sky-clad' in their rituals. Gardner was an enthusiastic naturist and, as Doreen Valiente writes, 'had a deep-rooted belief in the value of going naked when circumstances favoured it...' For him, she continues, 'communal nakedness, sunshine and fresh air were things which were natural and beneficial, both physically and psychologically.'[2]

Unfortunately, Gardner's other sexual tendencies found their way into his witchcraft practices as well. According to Francis King in *Ritual Magic in England,* 'Gardner was a sado-masochist with both a taste for flagellation and marked voyeuristic tendencies. Heavy scourging was therefore incorporated into most of his rituals and what Gardner called the "Great Rite" was sexual intercourse between the High Priest and the High Priestess while surrounded by the rest of the coven.'[3]

Crowley, of course, was an old hand at disguising references to sexual activity in his own ritual writings and had included similar allusions both in his *Book of Lies* and in *Magick in Theory and Practice.* With this in mind, it is not surprising that Crowley should have influenced Gardner as much as he did, for the two men obviously had much in common. Crowley's contribution to modern witchcraft, therefore, cannot be underestimated although, without doubt, most forms of neopaganism these days are decidedly more respectful to women than Crowley's cult of Babalon.

One of the reasons for this particular difference between Crowleyian magic and modern Wicca is the influence of other key figures in the witchcraft revival besides Gardner, including the American feminists, Janet and Stewart Farrar, and their original teacher — Alex Sanders.

Together with Gerald Gardner, Alex Sanders is widely regarded as one of the major figures in the contemporary witchcraft revival. He even has an entire tradition named after him, for Alexandrian witches — by virtue of a play on the words of his name — are those descended from his early initiatory covens in the late 1960s and early 1970s. This period was undoubtedly his heyday for he was then very much a public figure, and accompanied by his former wife Maxine, he gave witchcraft a ceremonial glamour.

These days, however, Alex Sanders lives in more modest circumstances, in a small seaside flat on the Bexhill promenade, but he has drawn around him a small coterie of friends and admirers. Now aged 68, he lives a life that in many ways appears drab and plain but when he dons his ceremonial masks and robes a very different persona emerges, and the magic of Alex Sanders is renewed.

By his own account Sanders was born in Manchester in 1916, although in his biography, *King of the Witches*, author June Johns gives the impression that he is perhaps ten years younger. This anomaly aside, it is clear that in the case of Alex

Sanders — a man who helped substantially to revive the worship of the Goddess in modern times — women played a major part in his upbringing. His mother, sister, and grandmother were the major forces in his early life, his often drunken and wayward father very much a lesser figure. According to June Johns, Sanders was raised on bread and dripping as a youth and the family had to struggle to make ends meet. Alex's mother Hannah was a cleaning lady, his father an itinerant musician. But it was his Welsh grandmother Grandma Bibby who was to determine young Alex's future occult career.

At the age of seven he happened one day to pay her an unannounced visit and came upon her naked 'with wrinkled belly and match-stick thighs', engaged in a witchcraft ritual in her kitchen. Sanders recalls that 'a number of curious objects surrounded her. There were swords, a black-handled knife, a sickle-shaped knife and various bowls lying around on the floor: other odd objects lay on a large Welsh dresser.'[4]

Frightened at first by this unexpected encounter, the lad was nevertheless sworn to secrecy by his grandmother and told he would be duly initiated. Grandma Bibby now ordered him to step forward into the magical circle, remove his clothes and bend over with his head between his thighs. Taking the sickle-knife in her hands she nicked Sanders' scrotum with it, drawing blood. 'You're one of us now,' she told him, and Sanders realized he was destined to be a witch.

In due course Grandma Bibby explained to her young grandson that she was descended from a line of witches dating back to the fourteenth-century Welsh chieftain Owain Glyn Dwr (Owen Glendower) who had worshipped the Great Goddess and kept the ancient Celtic traditions alive. Over the next few years a strong bond developed between Sanders and his grandmother, as she instructed him in making love potions and good luck charms, and also showed him the ceremony of 'drawing down the moon' — a ritual in which the High Priestess is transformed ceremonially into the living Lunar Goddess. He also learned how to write his own *Book of Shadows* — a private document handwritten by all practising witches, including ceremonies, invocations and charms, so called because its contents relate to the 'other world' of gods and spirits. Each *Book of Shadows* is very much an individual assortment of occult lore, and according to tradition is burnt when the old witch 'passes over'.

When Grandma Bibby died in 1942 Sanders destroyed her *Book of Shadows* in just this fashion but retained her black-handled knife, her sword, and other items of ritual equipment. Prior to her death she had initiated Sanders to the third degree, which included token sexual intercourse with her — an act symbolizing the union of the fertility goddess and her consort. So Sanders had a rich occult pedigree to offer to the world and now sought various ways of disseminating the techniques of witchcraft which he had learnt.

His initial forays into occult covens were characterized by materialistic self-advancement. By his own admission, Sanders engaged in ritual magic to bring about prosperity and sexual success — and it appeared to work. Sanders was taken up by a wealthy couple who for several years treated him as their son, bestowing all manner of gifts and riches upon him, and he also found himself at the heart of a frivolous, fun-loving group of promiscuous party-goers. This all had to come to an end, however, and in due course Sanders realized he had a more serious task ahead of him. He resolved to develop several witchcraft covens in the Manchester area and continue the work passed on to him by his grandmother.

It was during this time that he met Maxine Morris, an attractive blonde-haired teenager who had been raised as a devout Roman Catholic and educated at the local convent. Maxine's mother was a committed Christian but Maxine herself had had childhood visions of merging with the earth and sky, and Sanders was convinced she was a 'natural' witch. Although they were not drawn together at first they later realized a shared purpose, and married in 1967.

That same year Alex and Maxine moved to Notting Hill Gate and established the coven that in due course would attract Stewart and Janet Farrar to the path of witchcraft. By now Alex Sanders had established himself as the leading public witch in Britain and, just a few years earlier, had been endorsed by a group of 1623 practising wiccans as 'King of the Witches'. He was also becoming something of a media celebrity. There were numerous television appearances, late-night talks on the BBC, a forthcoming biography, record albums of his rituals, and even a film, *The Legend of the Witches*, based loosely on his pagan activities. Furthermore he was emphasizing an apparent point of superiority over Gerald Gardner — for Sanders had gained his third degree initiation from his grandmother whereas Gardner had only received his first degree from Old Dorothy. It is a point of distinction which still rankles in some occult circles when witchcraft pedigrees are discussed, for both Sanders and Gardner have large numbers of admirers and questions of 'authenticity', 'tradition' and 'lineage', as always, produce factionalism and rivalry. It is a difference which may never be resolved.

Sanders today is a far less flamboyant figure than he was when married to Maxine. The couple separated in 1973 and Sanders then drifted into semi-retirement in Bexhill. Maxine, meanwhile, continued her coven and still runs it today in

London, with a new consort and a distinctly low-key public presence.

However, the split also brought to the fore new elements in Alex Sanders' personality — aspects within him which for many years had lain dormant — and contact with occult forces beyond the realm of traditional witchcraft.

Earlier in life Alex had attended several meetings at spiritualist churches and seemed possessed of a healing power when laying-on-hands. Now, in Bexhill, he began developing contact with a discarnate force that could literally possess him in trance — the spirit of the Aztec.

Sanders first became interested in Aztec ritual in 1969 and began wearing a sumptuous pheasant-feather replica of Montezuma's war helmet in his ceremonial workings. At first Sanders noticed only subtle changes of mood but gradually the Aztec spirit of possession became much stronger, 'evolving its own character'. Sanders says that he resisted naming the spirit in order to tame its innate power, for he had found it to be potentially warlike and violent. At other times, however, it seemed benign, and able to offer a profound healing influence on those gathered in the group.

Sanders maintains that he is able to demonstrate 'mastery of Fire' and that he receives mediumistic messages from the magical planes. On these occasions Sanders 'passes responsibility' to the Aztec and the new persona takes over.

Watching the fire ceremony is impressive indeed. Aided by his magical colleagues Sanders dons his heavy mask and ritual gown and moves to the centre of his temple. There he disrobes and is handed two large, burning torches. In the next few minutes, accompanied by intense music which builds to a crescendo, the Aztec manifests through him — caressing his body with tongues of flame and leading Sanders' body through totally spontaneous physical gestures. Afterwards Sanders retains little memory of what has happened for in his role as a medium all conscious brain functions are placed in abeyance. For those vital minutes, the Aztec is totally in control.

Sanders believes that inner plane magic can affect the everyday world and that spirit possession is a valuable way of obtaining privileged information. He points to the concerted witchcraft activity in the New Forest directed against Hitler in the 1940s and maintains that he and his colleague, Derek Taylor, played a magical role in the recent Falklands War against the Argentine forces. For several months, says Sanders, he and Derek engaged in 'astral workings' in their temple and the effects were dramatic. He was able to deflect Exocet missiles from their targets, alter the outcome of decisive battles, and communicate with the spirits of deceased soldiers, one of whom, Bob Wilson, still speaks through him in mediumistic trance. On these occasions Derek serves as a scribe, writing down the messages as they are received.

Alex Sanders now looks back on his days of witchcraft with a sense of nostalgia although he has no regrets about his new direction. He would like to believe that he is still King of the Witches but, he says, somewhat flippantly, the women would never allow it — their role is now much more dominant in the movement than it used to be. Sanders, like Crowley and Gardner before him, belongs substantially to a different era. There was a time when, as his partner, Maxine was known as the Witch Queen. But kings and queens, and in fact lineages of all sorts, are fast becoming a thing of the past. What has emerged in their place is a deeply felt link with the earth and with Nature — a bond that is simultaneously an individual awakening and a shared consciousness among equals. In American neopaganism it has become especially clear that there is little role now for the rigid autocratic structures which characterized earlier occult movements. The mood instead has become one of positive change — away from hierarchy to a sense of personal transformation and self-renewal.

1. John Symonds, *The Great Beast*, 1973, p.43

2. Doreen Valiente, *An ABC of Witchcraft Past and Present*, 1973, p.156

3. Francis King, *Ritual Magic in England*, 1970, p.180

4. *Man, Myth and Magic*, 1970, issue number 40

CHAPTER 2

Wisdom from the Earth

She is in her mid-thirties, an impressive and enthusiastic woman with a mane of dark hair and a loud, infectious laugh. A reporter and interviewer for National Public Radio, she works in a congested office in downtown Manhattan and has a hectic schedule. She is also one of the leading spokespersons for neopaganism in America.

Margot Adler has impeccable credentials, both as a devotee of the magical arts and as a communicator. The granddaughter of distinguished psychiatrist Alfred Adler, Margot grew up in an intellectually rigorous Jewish family and went on to win a prestigious Neiman Fellowship at Harvard. She has left much of this behind her, however, and is most enthusiastic about the current upsurge in magical thinking. 'A new spirit of spiritual revolution is in the air...'

Margot has had a love of pagan traditions since she was twelve, when she 'fell in love' with the Greek gods and goddesses. In 1971 she was initiated into a Gardnerian witchcraft group and she is now a priestess with her own coven. She is also a very skilful writer and her book, *Drawing Down the Moon*, is widely regarded as the definitive overview of neopagan groups in the United States.

Expressive and exuberant, Margot feels a strong passion for her cause. Neopaganism, she says, has arisen because the orthodox religions are running out of steam and also, perhaps, because God is no longer at home in the mainstream Churches. People nowadays want to experience religion, not have it thrust at them in the form of a creed, and there is a distinct reaction against the sense of hierarchy in the Church. What appeals to Margot about witchcraft is its tribal nature, its direct relationship with the earth, and with the gods. There are no intermediaries, no pecking order. Influenced heavily by the experiential work at growth centres like Esalen Institute and the Human Potential movement in general, American neopaganism is turning tradition upside down and has a refreshing spontaneity. As Margot explains:

'I think that one of the reasons that so many people in the United States have come to paganism is that they see in it a way of resacralizing the world, of making it animated, of making it vivid again, of having a relationship to it that allows for harmony and wholeness. Perhaps this can help create a world that is more harmonious with Nature and can end the despoliation of the planet.'

There are strong political connotations here, of course, but also a profound mythological implication. For Margot Adler, paganism — and specifically goddess-oriented witchcraft — appeals because the creative energy of the earth is feminine. One of the major factors counting against the mainstream western religions is that their major orientation is male. Christianity has accorded the Virgin Mary a secondary role, and Judaism and Islam similarly focus on the male aspects of deity. Most people, says Margot, personify God as masculine and she quotes a famous saying from Mary Daly: 'If God is male, the male is God.' However, with the emergence of the feminist movement it is hardly surprising that many people, especially women, are turning to the feminine side of the godhead. 'The fundamental thing about the magical and pagan religions,' says Margot, 'is that ultimately they say: Within yourself *you* are the god, *you* are the goddess — you can actualize within yourself and create whatever you need on this earth and beyond. And therefore what is so subversive about the pagan religions, in a very powerful and beautiful way, is that women can realize: "You too are god." And that's a powerful message. Go into a feminist bookshop anywhere and you will find a whole shelf devoted to feminist spirituality — books, many of them, about witchcraft and paganism, many of them trying to reinterpret Christianity, reinterpret Judaism. There again is the creative, feminine energy. And it's brought many, many women into the pagan religions.'

There is also an increasingly political component in the pagan movement, although it is less accessible to outsiders. The Diablo Canyon nuclear power plant, located near San Luis Obispo on the beautiful Californian coast, provides a case in point. The power plant, as if by a grotesque sense of parody, has two dome-like structures which resemble breasts, and its physical presence is not only environmentally questionable — for it rests directly above the San Andreas fault — but, for the feminists, an insult to Mother Earth herself.

In 1981, another leading feminist, Miriam Simos — better known by her magical name of Starhawk — took her coven to Diablo Canyon for both a public blockade and a secret magical working. She was heartened by the fact that 'the anti-nuclear movement was organized much like witchcraft, around small, autonomous groups which have no hierarchy, work by consensus and give each other support'. Like many witches and occultists, Starhawk defines magic as 'the art of changing consciousness at will', and both at Diablo Canyon and more recently at the Lawrence Livermore Weapons Laboratory in Oakland, there have been magical hexing ceremonies aimed at negating the aggressive military consciousness promoted by the Reagan presidency.

Sceptics, of course, will regard such ritual activities as a sign of frustration — magic being summoned once rational debate becomes impossible — but it is interesting that there were several witches among the Greenham Common protesters in Britain and there is also an organization in Berkshire known as Pagans Against Nukes. Whether or not magical hexing is effective against the nuclear arms race may be questionable but the moral aspects of the issues addressed by paganism certainly make sense. As Starhawk says: 'Witchcraft has an inherent set of ethics because we view the earth and everyone on it, as valuable. We celebrate will that can cause change, and at the same time, we realize that we have to use it in balance, to create harmony not only in ourselves but in all life. When you see the world, the human community, and the diversity of life, as sacred, that gives you a strong push to go and do something to prevent it from being destroyed.'

Selena Fox and Jim Alan run the largest pagan network in the United States. Their quarterly newspaper *Circle Network News* has a print-run of 3000 and reaches a substantial section of the American pagan community, estimated variously at between 40,000 and 50,000 practising adherents.

Circle Sanctuary, which publishes the newsletter, operates from a rambling weatherboard house on a secluded 200-acre rural property west of Black Earth, Wisconsin. The land is a blend of fields and wooded hills but in one special place regal oaks and elegant silver birches form a cathedral-like canopy above a former Indian burial ground that is now the chosen site for magical 'stone circle' workings. Across the valley, and much higher up, is a marvellous stone ledge with commanding views of the whole property, while in the distance an inconspicuous dirt track winds its way up to the house through an avenue of trees.

Selena and Jim are not characteristic witches. She prefers not to use the term, calling herself instead a 'shamanic psychotherapist' or 'counsellor'. Jim, who rejected his orthodox Episcopalian background to become a pagan folksinger, agrees that the word 'witch' is unfortunate. It conjures to mind dark spells and medieval persecutions — as well as the inference that witchcraft is evil, whereas the Circle Sanctuary view of witchcraft is as a positive force in society. As Selena says, 'The magic we practise involves love, healing and helping, and we never use the force, the power, to harm anyone.'

Circle Sanctuary itself has an informal structure. Pagans may arrive from many different parts of the country to take part in seasonal rituals and there is a spontaneous, improvised quality in the Nature rituals which distinguishes them from the more formal aspects of traditional British witchcraft. Jim and Selena also co-ordinate several regional and national meetings, including the Pagan Spirit Gathering, which draws witches, magicians, shamans and goddess-worshippers from all areas of the United States, as well as other countries. 'We focus on unity and synthesis,' says Selena. 'We're working with the old in a new way. At our festivals, what connects us all is that we all honour Nature and care about healing the planet.'

Selena obviously enjoys the trappings of witchcraft and her life at home mirrors the archetypal image of the witch in fairytales and legends. She has a traditional witch's broom-

stick, handcrafted in Portugal, which serves both as an orna-
ment and as a ritual tool, and she scampers up and down stairs
with a characteristic 'witchy walk' as her long black hair
dances in the air. Her flashing eyes are dark and mischievous
and she chuckles as she mixes exotic broths and herbal teas
on the stove.

Despite her orthodox Baptist background, it is clear to her
that she was always headed for the mystical path. Raised in
a fundamentalist family in Arlington, Virginia, Selena had a
paranormal experience when she was only two years old,
floating 'out of her body' through the floorboards to another
room downstairs. Later, as a young child, she found herself
having prophetic dreams and seeing auras, but it wasn't until
she attended primary school that she discovered that the other
children didn't have experiences like this and didn't want to
talk about them.

After burying herself enthusiastically in writings like *The
Little Witch*, Selena graduated, at age 12, to her first book on
parapsychology — a work on extrasensory perception by
Professor J. B. Rhine. She remembers her youth as a time
spent developing harmony with Nature, especially in tending
her prized and much-loved flower and vegetable garden. Then
at 16, the crunch came. Urged by her family to give a sermon
before the Baptist congregation, she walked out declaring:
'God is not dead, but the Church is!' and became a committed
pantheist.

At the College of William and Mary — an institution with
the oldest educational charter in the United States — Selena
held her first pagan ritual: a Rites of Spring celebration in a
sunken garden that had been designed by Thomas Jefferson.
A classics professor at the College had found several authentic
Greek chants for her to sing and Selena put ivy in her hair and

led a pan-pipe procession, dancing and waving a phallic wand. While this was undoubtedly a sign of things to come, Selena had still not encountered contemporary witchcraft. That came in 1971, after she had graduated from college.

Selena was involved in an archaeological dig at Hampton, Virginia, and one of the other participants was a Prussian hereditary witch. Selena describes their meeting as 'like old sisters finding each other'. They performed ceremonies together, burnt candles and engaged in folk magic and moon worship.

Later Selena went to graduate school at Rutgers with the aim of becoming a social psychologist. But that also led to other things. Here she met a practitioner of folk magic, and she finally left the campus to live in his community in North Carolina, practising hexing and healing. At this time she also made contact with several other covens, but finally decided to work her magic on a private basis.

It was in 1973 that she met Jim Alan. She had come to Madison, Wisconsin, and was studying photography and commercial art. One day while she was meditating in her room she had an inner flash. She can remember it vividly, even now. 'I received a strong message saying there was a sign waiting for me on a telephone pole.' She went outside and there was an announcement for a psychic fair!

When she visited the gathering the next day she felt intuitively that she would meet someone who would be important to her. Walking through the crowd she came across a woman teaching automatic writing, and suddenly a 'flash' appeared above her head. Standing behind the woman was Jim Alan.

Jim and his brother Dennis also had had the feeling that the fair would produce an unexpected encounter. Jim was now 'open to occult intuitions' and had been involved with ritual magic, spiritualism and Tarot since 1968, before joining a coven in Milwaukee in 1970. He and Dennis had also studied astrology and the Kabbalah and were running an occult self-training group. Then they decided to co-ordinate the psychic fair in Madison — bringing together psychics, Tarot card readers, astrologers and palmists in a huge ballroom.

For Selena it wasn't simply a plunge into a new relationship. At Rutgers she had developed strong feminist convictions and she 'wasn't into being matched up'. However their feelings for each other grew steadily and several months later they became lovers. 'We were on top of a mountain . . . and it was as if dark veils between us had parted,' she recalls. A month later they handfasted as spiritual partners — a bond they still maintain at Circle Sanctuary.

At that time Jim's occult group was called Spectrum. It had six members who met weekly, and it encompassed Golden Dawn magic, Enochian chants, and ceremonial workings with robes, incense and candles. Circle Sanctuary emerged from Spectrum but with a much modified style and intent. Jim had been a folksinger for some time and he was now writing pagan songs as a tribute to the forces and rhythms of Nature. The approach was becoming less intellectual and more intuitive.

In 1976 Jim and Selena made their first public appearance at the Gnostica occult festival in Minneapolis, and the following year Circle developed as an outlet for publishing magical songs and lyrics. This soon blossomed into a succession of radio and television appearances and the beginnings of an extensive New Age networking system.

In 1977 Circle joined the Mid-West Pagan Council and the Pan Pagan Festival became an annual event. Several large festivals followed — some of them harmonious, but others troubled by problems between gays and straights, or between robed and 'sky-clad' practitioners of the Craft. As a result, Circle began to hold its own Pagan Spirit Gatherings in southern Wisconsin, coinciding with the summer solstice. In 1979 the confest attracted coverage in *Time* and *People* magazines and suddenly the movement was becoming public. There was perhaps no choice other than to plunge headlong into the media tide. After further radio and television appearances Circle gathered momentum as a national networking organization for the whole pagan movement. It still has this role and its magazine readership continues to grow.

Selena and Jim incorporated as a Church in Wisconsin in 1978 and later gained federal status. This entitles them to act as ministers, performing marriages and counselling community members in appropriate ways. However response to their cause in Wisconsin has been mixed.

As Jim explains:

'When we first purchased this land, word went out that we were involved in some kind of alternative religion and unfortunately some people thought we were a kind of mind-control cult or whatever, just because we were different. But as people got to know us, they realized that what we were doing was working with the earth in some of the same ways as they were. Our neighbours are farmers, and we're farmers, and we're farming and gardening on the land, and we very much love the land. We also seek to be in harmony not only with the land but with the neighbours around us.'

A characteristic ritual, performed by five members of the Circle on the site of the sacred burial mound, involves a purification ceremony followed by healing invocations. The stone circle on the mound was built during the winter solstice in 1983 from rocks on the property, and the ceremony begins as Selena sweeps the circle with her broom — an act of 'cleansing the sacred space'. Everyone present then holds ' hands and tunes in collectively to the woodlands all around. Then four members take cardinal positions on the periphery while Selena remains in the centre, and invocations are made to the spirits of the four quarters, beginning in the north and rotating clockwise. A group chant follows, and the effect is to build up a collective awareness. 'As we chant together,' says Selena, 'we feel ourselves connected with each other and with the space, and we imagine a light around the whole stone circle.' Calls are made to the animals on the land, and sacred yarrow flowers, which are symbolic of love and protection, are thrown into the ceremonial fire. Finally each member 'activates' the lines of force converging at the centre of the circle by visualizing a healing current in the earth as they walk in procession. The ritual ends with a visualization of a 'cone of power' which is lifted above the circle and then cast down into the earth as a healing blessing.

For Selena and Jim and the other members of the Circle group, the relationship with the land is of vital and central importance. Although in the popular imagination, witchcraft is considered to be mainly to do with spells and cackling crones, the reality is quite different. As Selena points out: 'We're working with the energies of the earth, and we're very much tuned into a love consciousness. We're seeking to do those kinds of things that religions around the world have as their essence, which is working with healing, working with love and working to achieve an inner balance.'

It is also significant — and characteristically different from British witchcraft — that the implements used in the ritual are not ornate ritual swords, cups and daggers, but objects which come from the land itself. The Circle ceremony uses rocks, twigs, flowers and herbs, and the invocations include a welcoming to the many animals on the property — foxes, deers, raccoons, possums, squirrels, red-tail hawks, eagles and owls. Selena and Jim are profoundly respectful of the fact that the American Indians, probably Chippewa or Objibwa, revered this land and its co-habitants, and they are keen to continue the tradition in their own way. 'Circle Sanctuary,' says Selena, 'is sacred land purchased to be held by pagans for use by pagans.'

'After all,' she adds, 'Mother Nature is the greatest teacher.'

In England and Ireland witchcraft draws on more specific traditions than in the United States and witches, as we have already seen, have been more inclined to claim lineages and other particular types of 'authenticity'. For example, the influential English witch, Patricia Crowther, who heads a coven in Sheffield, was initiated into the Craft by Gerald Gardner in 1960, four years before his death. She emphasizes secrecy and strongly opposes witches who 'break their oaths' and release too much information to the public. Accordingly, for her, the 'old school' of witches — including Doreen Valiente, Lois Bourne and Eleanor Bone — are authentic, whereas many of the more public witches 'have not been properly initiated'.

Janet and Stewart Farrar, especially, have had to face criticisms of this kind. To a large extent they have assumed Alex Sanders' former role and are now among the most visible practitioners of contemporary witchcraft. They have also written two major works together, *Eight Sabbats for Witches* and *The Witches' Way*, recently published in the United States as the two-volume *Witches' Bible*. The rituals, spell-craft and specific conjurations described in these books represent a working guide to practical witchcraft and provide the sort of information Patricia Crowther believes should remain strictly for the inner circle.

Both Janet and Stewart, however, are frank and open about their occult beliefs and practices, and about how they came to the Craft.

Janet was raised in East London in a strictly Christian family and her grandfather was a church councillor in their Anglican parish. However she began to drift away from Christianity during her adolescent years and later became briefly involved in Transcendental Meditation. Meanwhile she was working as a model and then became a secretary in the Beatles' London office.

Around this time she visited Alex and Maxine Sanders' coven in Notting Hill Gate. She was impressed by Wicca as a spiritual path and decided to join. It was here that she met her husband Stewart, who was visiting simply as a journalist for *Reveille* magazine. Despite the fact that he is now twice her age — she is 34 years old, he 68 — they were drawn together as magical partners and were both initiated in 1970 — Janet by Alex, and Stewart by Maxine. This follows the general Craft principle that a man should initiate a woman and a woman, a man.

In 1975 Janet and Stewart married, both in a traditional Wiccan ceremony and in a registry office — and the following year moved to southern Ireland, where Stewart was able to gain tax-relief as an author of science-fiction novels, his other major interest.

Janet and Stewart now run their own coven from a secluded country farm-house near Drogheda, north of Dublin. The lifestyle is admittedly rustic and uncomplicated. An ongoing procession of dogs and farm animals parades through the house, the living room serves as a pagan gathering place, and more often than not is filled with cigarette smoke and used coffee cups. Janet and Stewart like to be surrounded by people and thrive on the feeling of pagan community. Also living with them in the house are Janet's father — a practising Christian who is tolerant of her pagan beliefs — and other members of the coven, including a middle-aged Australian woman, Jane Russell, and her daughter Ginny. The animal retinue currently comprises 15 cats, four dogs, two ponies, a donkey, two dozen chickens and five ducks.

Janet and Stewart like to live close to Nature and feel their main purpose is to develop psychic powers for healing and self-knowledge. In most of their rituals they work 'sky-clad' because they feel it is more natural, and also because it helps to raise psychic power. Stewart explains:

'Witches at work bring all levels into operation — spiritual, mental, astral, etheric, physical... Trying to work with one of them screened is like trying to play the piano in gloves, or painting a picture wearing dark glasses.' He also says that ritual nudity is more compatible with self-development:

'There is nothing so image-forming as clothes. It is a great symbolic step in the direction of being yourself and discovering who you are if you discard them. It is also more democratic. We have had in our coven at the same time an Indian princess and a building worker, and as the labourer put it, "When we've got our clothes off in the circle, we are just people." '

Typical of their ritual workings is the initiation of Francis de Venney, a young and aspiring member of their coven. The ritual combines ancient symbolism with Stewart's gift for scriptwriting.

At the outset Francis receives instructions from Janet that he will undergo an ordeal similar to the traditional quest followed by the Celtic warriors of old — through Earth, Air, Water and Fire. As his prize Francis will become fully initiated into first degree membership of the Craft.

Francis is led to an apparently remote location in the Irish countryside[1] and is then disrobed. Bound at the wrists and ankles, he is blind-folded with a gag around his mouth, and is then left curled up in a foetal position at the foot of a hawthorn tree. Throughout his experience he will be called on by Ginny, who addresses him by his magical name, 'Usna'.

Freezing cold as he lies on the frosty ground, Francis struggles to loosen the bonds from his ankles and now finds himself sliding clumsily through leaf-strewn gullies and mud puddles. Overcoming the ordeal of Earth he runs blindfold through an open paddock, painfully embracing Air as the cold December wind brushes against his body.

Although he does not know it, Francis is gradually being led back to the homestead. Most of the coven members, including Janet, have now returned to prepare for the welcoming ceremony while Ginny draws him still nearer with her calls. Stewart, garbed in ritual robes and his magnificent horned crown, watches Usna's progress with interest from behind a hedgerow.

Still blindfolded, Francis now has to cross a freezing stream. Ginny calls out to him: 'Water is the element of your heart, your love and compassion, of loyalty and self-sacrifice. Your lips are unbound so that you may now speak what is in your heart...'

Freeing himself from the gag, Francis stumbles to the further bank and is now drawn closer to the house — where a fire-ordeal has been prepared. Ginny releases Usna's blindfold and his task is to run nimbly through an irregular course of tall, flaming torches. Hesitant at first, he leaps forward, weaving past the flickering tongues of fire to the doorway of the house.

Inside, the temple-room is illuminated by an open fire. An altar nearby is lit with candles, and a large mural of the Mother Goddess adorns the wall behind it. Stewart, who has disrobed but still wears the horned crown of the High Priest, welcomes Usna at the door and leads him into the coven. Stewart now invokes the God of the Sacred Oak:

'Thou God of Old, thou mighty Horned One, thou who dwelt upon the waters and wert the first light of dawn — return to us again. Come at our call by rushing winds and leaping flame...'

Usna now stands before Janet, who personifies the energies of the lunar Goddess. She wears a skirt of silver, a crown of bright jewels, and is naked to the waist.

Stewart says to Usna: 'Behold and welcome our Lady, the Goddess of the Moon!' Janet now greets the new initiate in Gaelic, as several other members of the coven form a circle around them. Another member beats a bodhran, and the witches hasten their tempo, moving faster and faster in a clockwise direction and chanting passionately as they dance. As it is all coming to a climax, Janet plunges her ritual athame into a chalice held high by Stewart and all members of the coven then kiss and embrace. The celebration, as always, ends with a 'feast'.

For the members of the coven the ritual is a mythic event, encompassing the five elements of creation and the god-forms of an ancient pantheon. As Stewart is keen to point out, the male god of the witches, Cernunnos, is always shown with horns and has been wrongly associated with the horned goat of the medieval Satanists. Explaining a reference from the Old Testament, Stewart notes that 'horns are an ancient symbol of divine power'. However, unlike orthodox Judaism with its patriarchal emphasis, Wicca is a matriarchal religion. For this reason Janet, as High Priestess, has the paramount role in the coven and Stewart serves as consort to the 'reigning Queen'.

As has already been pointed out by Margot Adler, this distinction certainly has contemporary appeal. Janet explains:

'Once a woman realizes her own psychic potential she becomes fully mature and can reunite man with herself in a way that mankind hasn't seen for aeons. We don't want to *replace* a male-dominated culture with a female-dominated one. We want to make the two work in perfect harmony.'

As one would expect with sky-clad ceremonies sexuality plays a major role in modern witchcraft, although in most instances as a reflection of polarity and balance rather than as a display of hedonistic indulgence. For Janet and Stewart, Wicca is based on the complementary roles of male and female, both in ritual procedure and as a bonding force between magical partners. Sexual magic is usually performed only between established lovers, or between husband and wife, and in private rather than with the group.[2] However, when acts of this type do take place, it is invariably within the magical circle. Witches will often consummate marriage or try to conceive a child within the circle of their temple, because they feel that if a child is going to be born into a Wiccan family then it should be conceived 'in the presence of the gods'.

Like their American counterparts, Janet and Stewart Farrar regard witchcraft as an alternative religion, a path which leads to a balance of the spiritual with the mental and physical dimensions of our existence. As with the witches of Circle Sanctuary in Wisconsin, the Drogheda coven is strongly conservationist and environmental in its outlook, for Nature, herself, is sacred. 'The world at the moment needs an injection of the pagan outlook,' says Janet. 'This means relating to the earth, relating to the environment, relating to our fellow creatures. We are in danger of losing that contact and the balance needs restoring. Culture, religion and society have been male-dominated for two thousand years or more, and life has got out of balance. We need to recover the feminine aspect — the Goddess.'

In Australia, modern witchcraft has had a very different history. Here it was the controversy aroused through works of supernatural art that led to interest in paganism and earned witchcraft a mixed reputation.

For most Australians in the post-war generation, Rosaleen Norton was the first witch they had ever heard of. An exotic and bohemian artist, she aroused a considerable public outcry by exhibiting paintings of naked gods and goddesses, proclaiming her allegiance to the Great God Pan, and describing herself as 'the Witch of Kings Cross' — a reference to Sydney's colourful red-light district.

Rosaleen Norton was born in Dunedin, New Zealand in 1917 and migrated with her family to Sydney when she was still a child. As early as the age of three she had been drawing ghosts and shining dragons, and as a precocious secondary-school student she alarmed her fellow pupils with her drawings of vampires, ghouls and werewolves.

After being expelled by her headmistress for her 'corrupting' influence on the other children, young Rosaleen studied art at East Sydney Technical College and then took a job with *Smith's Weekly* as a writer and junior artist. Eighteen months later she abandoned this to become a pavement artist and studio model, working also as a waitress in night clubs and as a designer for a toy manufacturer.

A drawing by Rosaleen Norton

When she was 23 she had her first mystical experience —
'a feeling of disintegration and ecstasy' in which her spirit
seemed to soar into the sky before returning to her body again.
This led her to explore the available literature on magic,
trance states, comparative religions and Jungian psychology.
She soon became totally intrigued by the potential of the
human mind.

Rosaleen was now drawing pictures of the gods and spirits
she was contacting in trance. Sometimes she would spend

several days in a state of dissociation, guarded by her sister Cecily, and then return to capture her visions on canvas. The result was an exhibition of paintings which would earn her public notoreity almost overnight.

In 1949 Rosaleen's work came to the attention of Professor Oeser, then head of the department of psychology at the University of Melbourne. An exhibition of her paintings was arranged and Rosaleen was interviewed for her thoughts on trance states, her exploration of the subconscious, and her contact with what she called 'god-forms'. She was evaluated as having a 'schizophrenic personality' but also very high intelligence. However, it was her art that made the most impact of all. Critics who visited the exhibition were horrified by her paintings which had titles like 'Merlin', 'The Gnostic', 'The Initiate' and 'Pan' — and they described them variously as 'stark sensuality running riot', 'the result of a nightmare-dipped brush' and 'as gross a shock to the average spectator as a witch's orgy'. Accused of producing pornography, she was now experiencing public wrath for the first time. But she was a match for her critics. 'Obscenity', she countered, 'like beauty, is in the eye of the beholder. This figleaf morality expresses a very unhealthy attitude.'

Rosaleen returned to her life as a bohemian artist in Kings Cross and it was just a few years later, accompanied by poet Gavin Greenlees, that she met journalist and editor, Walter Glover. Apalled by their 'squalid circumstances' Glover offered to finance Rosaleen's art with a view to publishing it some day in book form, and this led, in due course, to the publication in 1952 of *The Art of Rosaleen Norton*. It was a handsome limited edition, bound in red leather and embossed with gold lettering, but like Rosaleen's earlier exhibition in Melbourne it provoked a fierce outcry from the media. Newspapers around the country denounced the book as 'the most blatant example of obscenity yet published in Australia' and the Post Master General threatened prosecution for registering an indecent publication.

These days the works of Rosaleen Norton seem harmless enough. Admittedly, a strong pagan current runs through her work, there are hints of both evil and visionary excitement in her compositions, and many of the gods and spirits depicted are naked. But the public reaction to her paintings in the 1950s was out of all proportion to their content. It was as if a deep pagan pulse had been tapped and mainstream morality was offended.

Walter Glover came before a magistrate and was fined five pounds plus costs. But far worse than this, the book had drained his resources. Within a few years he was in a state of financial ruin.

Rosaleen, meanwhile, had become a national celebrity and a spate of magazines now ran gaudy headlines announcing exclusive interviews with an authentic pagan witch. This new-found curiosity in her work allowed Rosaleen to explain to the public her belief in pantheism, in the ongoing 'reality' of the ancient gods, and the value of Nature-worship. There were further court-cases and accusations of obscenity, but the point had been made. A deep occult current had bubbled to the surface in seamy Kings Cross.

Rosaleen Norton found an interesting ally, however, in the distinguished musician Sir Eugene Goossens — at that time Conductor of the Sydney Symphony Orchestra. Perhaps bored by his staid and conservative work colleagues, he found Rosaleen and Gavin exciting to be with, and joined the small witchcraft coven they had established in Kings Cross. But controversy erupted yet again when Sir Eugene returned to

Sydney airport from an overseas trip, laden with ceremonial tribal masks and pagan art-objects. Customs officials were intrigued by the nature of his purchases and wondered what use they could possibly have: it was not long before he was dismissed from his post at the Conservatorium of Music and obliged to return to England. Rosaleen, meanwhile, continued with her bohemian lifestyle, painted numerous occult murals on the walls of coffee-shops and restaurants in Kings Cross, and became a celebrated and well known eccentric. She died in a hospice in December 1979.

It is fair to say that Australian witchcraft has not seen such a colourful and exotic pagan personality since Rosaleen's death, but covens continue to flourish in several Australian cities, especially Sydney and Perth. Most witches keep to themselves, meet on the sabbats and take a low public profile. There are several small occult magazines, like *Kindred Spirits Quarterly*, *The Source* and *Shadowplay* which allow pagans to keep in touch with each other, but the witchcraft movement as a whole remains informal and de-centralized; very much a case of individuals doing their own thing.

One of the better known covens in Australian witchcraft is based in Perth. Comparable in style to the groups established by Alex Sanders in the 1960s, it is still somewhat hierarchical and continues to emphasize the idea of magical lineage — a feature noticeably less prevalent in American neopaganism. The Coven of Lothlorien, however, has two strong personalities at the helm, which goes some way to explaining its structure.

Now aged 40, Gwydyon is a well built, handsome man of German extraction. He is High Priest of the coven and shares an equal role with his wife, Lady Tanith. Both are professional entertainers by day — specializing in a spectacular fire-eating act which has taken them on tour as far afield as Las Vegas. But their witchcraft is also a major part of their lives and, like the Farrars, they take a keen responsibility for the welfare of other members of their group.

Gwydyon was born in Victoria and learnt a blend of Freemasonry and magic from his father. He had another teacher as well — Gwydyon prefers that he remain anonymous — and this person had trained with Dion Fortune: a leading English occultist and psychotherapist who had been a member of one of the splinter orders descended from the Golden Dawn. There is no doubt that Gwydyon likes to feel he is carrying on an occult tradition and that he can share this knowledge now with the other members of the coven.

After a variety of occupations, including working as a paramedic on the Bass Strait oil-fields and later as an ambulance driver, Gwydyon came to Perth in 1971 and met Tanith four years later.

She was an émigré from Scotland, a vivacious and cheerful woman with rich amber hair and a colourful personality. Her background was quite different to his. Educated in a convent and brought up as a strict Roman Catholic, she had deserted the fold by marrying a Jehovah's Witness, but the marriage was shortlived and she found herself looking for a new perspective. Her first contact with the occult — books on astral travel and witchcraft — 'terrified' her but she was intrigued by spiritualism and the interpretation of dreams. When she met Gwydyon she was still not sure whether Wicca was really some form of devil-worship — her religious upbringing had warned her specifically against encounters of this type. However Tanith says that, at heart, she was really goddess-oriented and it was comparatively easy switching from the Virgin Mary to the White Goddess. And her personal attraction to Gwydyon was also very strong. She was totally drawn to him — even if he was a witch!

Gwydyon became Tanith's manager, arranging her fire-eating engagements, and the couple also started an occult shop, The Sorceress, in Fremantle. They had now formed a coven and were alternating their evenings between floor shows and Craft workings, as well as ordering stocks of incense, books and ritual equipment for the shop.

Gwydyon and Tanith agree that their coven is unconventional, even a little conservative. Tanith says she does not like to take the dominant role for herself — preferring an 'equal polarity' between Gwydyon and herself. While she is not, herself, a feminist, she does see her role primarily as 're-awakening the Goddess' for members of her group. However she recognizes Gwydyon's considerable knowledge of magic, witchcraft and the Kabbalah, and many of the distinctive aspects of the coven are more due to his influence than to hers. Gwydyon calls his orientation Modern Wicca — a blend of witchcraft and Kabbalistic magic — and there is also a Celtic flavour to many of the rituals. But there is a strong martial arts input as well — a reflection of Gwydyon's personal interest in Kung Fu and Ninja techniques. All members of the coven have some acquaintance with Bando Banshay, a Burmese form of Kung Fu, and Gwydyon maintains this is particularly useful because the 'warrior priest' was an important role in ancient Celtic tradition. All rituals performed in their temple room therefore include a guard armed with a spear, and this figure also personifies the idea of 'psychic defence' — maintaining the spiritual integrity of the ritual.

The Coven of Lothlorien divides its three Wiccan initiations into eighteen-month periods and members learn not only about Wicca but also about Celtic mythology, Egyptian magic and the Kabbalah, as well as how to conduct wiccanings and handfastings. The coven, they say, is a family and the lives of all the participants interconnect on a social as well as on a magical level.

Gwydyon believes it is not without reason that Perth is known as the 'City of Light', for there are more occultists in this city per capita of population than in any city in the southern hemisphere! He is convinced there is an ongoing occult revival:

'In the last nine years, Wicca in Perth has expanded considerably. All of the original members of our coven are now running their own groups ... and with very few exceptions all the people that we've assisted in putting through the Craft have worked very hard to establish a coven and help build the movement in a positive way.'

But the Coven of Lothlorien also has its problems — and these have mostly to do with stereotyping and cheap publicity in the media. They still get mistaken for Satanists:

'The Sunday press finds it easy to sell papers if they can mix sex, drugs and nudity under the usual heading of witchcraft — "The wicked in the West". Because the way we work has been secret for so long, people are very suspicious.'

Admittedly many of the Wiccan practices, especially spellcraft, do look a little odd and could easily be mistaken for fetish worship or black magic.

One of these rituals involves forming a small doll from clay and then connecting it with a cord to Tanith's mouth. Symbolically this brings life from the Great Mother, and the doll represents the principle of welcoming life from the earth. The doll is drawn down over the High Priestess' womb, which as Gwydyon explains, 'is the ancient altar in the matriarchal faiths', and the figurine is then used in a magical ceremony to focus the coven's powers of healing. But as in all types of magic, the symbolic form is simply representative of something broader and more intangible: in this case the mysteries of the creation of life and the emergence of mankind from 'the dust of the earth'.

Spells, says Gwydyon, can be used for both positive and negative magic but in this case the intent is a positive one. 'Spells can be used to help, heal, bless or hinder. The Wiccan spell, the witch's spell, the blessing — these are no different to a church's blessing. The spells we do are simply to help someone... a blessing is a good spell.'

If Gwydyon and Tanith, and the Reverend Gordon Melton are right, however, Wicca still has a long way to go before its integrity is established in the eyes of the public. For most people the witch is still a sinister figure, a strange being performing even stranger rituals in the shadows of a dusty room. It is an image which even the witches of the City of Light will find difficult to eradicate.

1. Francis is unfamiliar with the location but in fact it is within walking distance of his home.

2. In the third degree of modern witchcraft there may be sexual intercourse between High Priest and High Priestess but coven members leave the circle.

CHAPTER 3
Awakening the Goddess

As we have seen, the Goddess looms large in the occult, especially in Wicca. The idea of goddess-worship, however, is a larger concept than coven-based witchcraft, and its rituals are broader in scope, more diverse, and less bound by the traditional Wiccan concept of a three-fold initiation. Most goddess-worshippers do not refer to themselves as witches for, in its broadest interpretation, this form of belief is a universal feminist religion, drawing on mythologies from many different ancient cultures. And the idea of God-as-woman finds expression in many different places — as far afield as Berkeley, California, Clonegal Castle in southern Ireland, and the Yanchep caves of Western Australia.

Z Budapest (pronounced Zee) is one of the most famous of all contemporary goddess-worshippers and also one of the most vitriolic. In her view feminine spirituality has been disregarded for hundreds of years in the West because of Christianity and male dominance of cultural trends. Nevertheless, she perceives that things are changing and she wants very much to be part of it. As feminism broadens its scope to extend beyond socio-economic and political realms, a new type of spiritual transformation is underway. 'I feel,' says Z, 'that the women's movement is badly in need of energizing. To reclaim our souls is the next step in achieving the goals of the movement, after taking back our bodies...'

Zsuzsanna Budapest was born in Hungary in 1940, the daughter of a psychic medium. Zsuzsanna's mother, Masika Szilagyi, conceived poems of invocations while in trance and apparently sometimes spoke in ancient Egyptian. She was also an artist, poet and Tarot reader and earned recognition in Budapest as a sculptoress of note — often featuring pagan and goddess themes in her motifs. Most importantly for Z, her mother also had an impeccable pedigree as a Taltos shamaness, and could trace her mystical lineage back to the fourteenth-century pagan King Mätyas. Part of Z's dislike for the medieval Christian church stems from the fact that in Hungary, Christianity put an end to the pagan culture. It is now one of Z's central aims to restore it.

Z lives in Oakland, California, a few blocks from the city centre, but she has lived and worked in many parts of the United States. At the age of 19 she came to Illinois from Vienna, where she had been studying languages, and renewed her interest in German literature at the University of Chicago. Later she worked in theatre in New York, studying techniques of improvisation, and in 1970 she went west to Los Angeles.

It is on the west coast that she has made most of her impact, proclaiming her pagan heritage and stimulating interest in 'women's mysteries' within the feminist movement. Soon after arriving in Los Angeles she opened a now legendary occult shop, the Feminist Wicca, on Lincoln Boulevarde in Venice. This store served as a 'matriarchal spiritual centre', dispensing candles, oils, incense, herbs, jewellery, Tarot cards and other occult paraphernalia, and it also emerged as a meeting place for women wishing to perform rituals together. Soon there were groups of witches meeting for ceremonies on the equinoxes and solstices and, as Z says, 'feminist spirituality had been born again'.

Among the best known of her friends at this time was Miriam Simos, a softly spoken Jewish girl who had rejected yoga and Buddhism as 'male authoritarian'. After graduating from UCLA and studying feminism, Miriam heard about Z's centre and became interested in the public rituals to the goddess Diana which were being performed there. Now known by her magical name, Starhawk, Miriam has written two highly regarded books, *The Spiral Dance* and *Dreaming the Dark*, both of which are key works in the revival of goddess-worship.

Starhawk lost contact with Z for a time after moving north to form her own coven in San Francisco. Meanwhile Z was attracting a new type of fame through the media.

On 10 February 1975, Z was arrested and charged with fortune-telling after giving an undercover policewoman a Tarot card reading. Prior to going on trial in West Los Angeles, she announced at a press club meeting that her supporters would be burning 2000 candles 'on altars throughout the city'. Describing herself as the 'first witch to go on trial for her beliefs in 300 years' Z proclaimed herself to be a religious leader and demanded her right to freedom of belief under the First Amendment. This was partly to rebuke her legal charge, since fortune-telling was forbidden under the Municipal Code unless performed by a religious leader. Z maintained strongly that she deserved this exempt status, noting that she was now High Priestess of the Susan B. Anthony #1 Coven — a group named after a controversial nineteenth-century suffragette.

The trial resulted in a $300 fine and a probation order forbidding Z to read Tarot cards, so she turned instead to supplementing her income by *teaching* classes in Tarot, divination and witchcraft — a change of emphasis allowed for under the law.

Z's brush with the authorities did nothing to diminish her outspokenness, however, and many people who had heard of her through the media were now intrigued to know what sort of religion she practised. In a lengthy interview with journalist Cheri Lesh[1], published shortly after the trial, Z explained that Wicca was not inverted Christianity but represented the remnants of a much older, matriarchal system of worship which recognized the feminine as the creative force in Nature. In the interview Z spoke of the bloody transition from a matriarchal society to a patriarchal form, in which roaming bands of warriors ravaged the great Queendoms of Anatolia, Sumer and Thrace and fragmented the 'Great Goddess' into a number of minor deities. This led to a much diminished status for the goddesses, who by now had confined and restricted roles. In Greek mythology, for example, Aphrodite became simply a goddess of love and sexuality, while Artemis represented hunting, and Athena wisdom. Hera, Amphitrite and Persephone, meanwhile, became adjuncts to Zeus, Poseidon and Hades (Pluto).

As Z Budapest pointed out, such a transition was a major cultural disaster:

'Mythology is the mother of religions, and grandmother of history. Mythology is human-made, by the artists, storytellers, and entertainers of the times. In short, culture-makers are the soldiers of history, more effective than guns and bombers. Revolutions are really won on the cultural battlefields.'

Z maintained that the impact was far-reaching:

'Women understand this very well, since we became aware of how women's culture had been ripped off by the ruling class. This resulted in a stunted self-image of women, which resulted in insecurities, internalizing the cultural expectations of us created by male culture-makers. Most of the women in the world still suffer from this spiritual poverty.'

A second major disaster occurred in Britain and Europe between the fourteenth and seventeeth centuries, when witch-hunting hysteria was mounted by the Inquisition. In her interview Z Budapest characterized Christianity as a death-worshipping religion with its focus 'centred on a dead, bleeding god on a cross'. The Great Goddess, by way of contrast, had been worshipped in acts of love and rejoicing, and that was the way it should be. Z still blames the medieval Church for confusing witchcraft and Satanism, and giving them both a bad name:

'Witchcraft is a universal, joy-oriented, artistic kind of religious practice that celebrates the earth and its journey around the sun. Now we got a bad rap from the Christians about this. We have been told that we worship Satan, the Devil. Well, the Devil is a Christian god. We have never heard of the Devil. Many of us got burned because we didn't know who they were talking about...So many died. Many were going to their death still wondering who the Devil was...'

Not surprisingly, Z's form of Dianic worship excludes men altogether. She says, somewhat dismissively, that if the men wish to discover the 'inner woman' within themselves, they can join an occult movement known as the Radical Fairies — a group whose name has somewhat unfortunate connotations. The women's mysteries, as Z sees them, must be kept pure and strong, and men have no place in them. As she succinctly puts it, 'We have *women's* circles. You don't put men in

71

women's circles — they wouldn't be women's circles anymore.'

'Our Goddess is Life,' she adds, 'and women should be free to worship from their ovaries.'

Z now favours an equal mix of lesbian and heterosexual women in her circles to 'balance the polarities' in her rituals. She is a practising lesbian herself although she has not always been that way inclined. Z was married in an earlier phase of her life and now has two sons in their twenties — one a physicist, the other a fighter pilot with the marines. However, she is very much an active feminist now, and has chosen to deliberately avoid what she calls the 'duality' of man and woman. In more orthodox heterosexual witchcraft circles, she argues, the women tend to perform for the men. Her new emphasis on women's mysteries keeps the tradition pure and strong. It also allows the different phases of womanhood to be honoured in their own right: the young, the mature and the old woman each have much to offer and in Z's group, cere-monies are performed for each of these phases of life.

Currently there is increasing input from the Native Amer-ican Indian tradition and at any one of the ritual gatherings the ceremonial garb is likely to include feathered head-dresses and Indian beads as well as the more familiar flowing robes, lunar crowns and pentagrams. Z is also affiliated with many talented goddess-worshippers who are High Priestesses in their own right and have their own private sanctuaries as well as working in groups.

One of these is Maud Reinertsen, who has lived in Berkeley for many years. Maud arrived in 1968, recently divorced, with her young daughter, and felt a strong sense of anger about the direction her life was taking. In her own words, she was 'looking for the revolution'. Instead she was shown a Tarot deck by a friend and became interested in occult symbolism. Initially she had regarded magical practices as evil and weird — which was hardly surprising since her parents were Episcopalian missionaries in Africa. However, through the Tarot she discovered a rich mythology, and was also impressed by the many facets of the Goddess which were present in the Major Arcana, the pictorial cards of the deck.

Maud came to the view that the ideal religious expression focused on a Goddess who personified sex as a 'healthy, sacred act'. While she had previously 'felt bad' about her body, the sky-clad ceremonies in goddess-worship broke down some of her inhibitions and she felt a sense of self-renewal.

Maud now runs a Temple of the Goddess from her rented home and is also an 'astrological consultant'. 'Astrology,' she says, 'is an ancient psychology.' She likes to join periodically with fellow goddess-worshippers but keeps a reasonably low public profile. Her neighbours simply wouldn't understand.

Luisah Teish is another friend and fellow worshipper in Z's circle, and brings a quite different perspective to the ceremonial workings, for her background combines the Nigerian Yoruba tradition and southern Voodoo. An attractive, exotic black woman with large, expressive eyes and a broad, beaming smile, Luisah has magic in her blood and it shows as she dances, chants, and invokes the gods of her heritage.

Now in her late thirties, Luisah was born in New Orleans of mixed African, Haitian, Native American and French ancestry. She was raised as a 'Louisiana Catholic' — a polite expression for one who practises Voodoo with a thin veneer of Christianity over the top.

It wasn't a case of deliberately pursuing magic, says Luisah, so much as waiting for it to happen. The elders would perform secret rites around her as she was growing up and watch for omens, or for significant traits to emerge in her personality. Luisah's mother wanted her to be a nurse or teacher, and would ignore her questions about 'women's mysteries'. Nevertheless Luisah found she had an innate capacity for prophetic dreams and would frequently sleepwalk. She learnt magical cures by fossicking around for bits of information, and also gleaned insights into occult ways of reading weather patterns and interpreting animal behaviour. Luisah explained that there is a paranoid element among Voodoo practitioners in the deep south because practising traditional African religion on the slave-plantations was punishable by death. Voodoo instead became incorporated into domestic routine that wouldn't be noticed by the slave owners.

Luisah recounts a fascinating event from her youth:

'When I was a little girl my mother used to send me to the Catholic church and she would tell me, "Go and ask Father Fitzpatrick for a little holy water." You know, she'd send me with a jar and I'd go get the holy water from the church, and she'd put it in a bucket with sugar, urine and a little perfume. Then she'd get a picture of one of the saints and mop the floor, and the whole time she was mopping the floor she was telling the saint what she wanted to have happening in her house — magically, that is. That's what I call being "Louisiana Catholic", where you're Catholic on the surface but there's a lot more going on underneath.'

When she was in her early twenties Luisah decided to confront her mother about her magical practices by tricking her into becoming a confidante. Luisah announced that she was going to make a magical charm with graveyard dust. Her mother clearly recognized that Luisah was ready for the secrets, and confided to her daughter that she was a medium and a member of an 'altar circle'. They have been 'good buddies' ever since.

Luisah inherited two magical traditions — New Orleans Voodoo and the *Lucumi* Yoruba religion of Nigeria. She is now a priestess of Oshun, the Nigerian counterpart of the Roman goddess Venus, who is known also as 'Mother of the Spirit'. According to Luisah the Goddess lies asleep in the crown chakra — the psychic energy centre in the head. When a person is ritually initiated the magical herbs and songs arouse the spirit, and the devotee is possessed by the Goddess. According to Luisah, 2000 people in the Bay Area around San Francisco practise some form of Voodoo or Macumba, its Brazilian counterpart. However, many are still afraid to admit it publicly.

Luisah's magic is mostly benevolent and people come to her primarily for spiritual advice, or for wealth and love charms. Luisah claims to be able to reverse black magic, but rarely inflicts harmful magic on others. 'Before doing that,' she says with a grin, 'I'd have to check with the gods first.'

For Luisah, as for several other members of the group, magical dance in the Goddess ceremony has a very powerful effect. As Luisah explains, for her it induces a state of trance possession and also the feeling of being out-of-the-body:

'Suddenly I find I'm dancing off-rhythm, and an ancestor or a spirit is there. You are bombarded by music, and not really in control of your body. It seems that the drummer's hands are your feet and then at some point there is a great silence. You find you are now on the wall, on the ceiling — over there somewhere — watching your body performing. And the spirit begins to ride you like a horse...

'Usually after a ceremony I clearly feel that my feet are a few inches above the ground and I have to deliberately stomp to remind myself that I'm here right now.'

For Luisah, the ceremony takes her into a completely different state of awareness:

'It's very invigorating. The body seems to be able to do things in trance that you cannot do when you're fully conscious. Bursts of energy come in and take over. It's wonderful... I love it!'

Z has a similar feeling about the Goddess invocations in the magical circle. For her the rituals have a healing, integrating effect:

'I feel that my life has meaning, that something I can say and do makes me feel good and everybody else feel good. The circles leave me high and for days afterward I still feel energized. A permanent smile forms on my face when I remember the happy times under the Moon and I can feel the stars on my face...'

Thousands of miles away across the Atlantic, in the little Irish village of Clonegal, a similar revival of goddess-worship is taking place.

One comes to Clonegal by a meandering country road, flanked by hedgerows and rolling fields. The closest township is Bunclody, with its charming market square and sloping main street. Away to the north, some two hours' drive away, lies the clutter of Dublin, but here the mood is tranquil and timeless. The narrow road into Clonegal passes across a humped stone bridge, veers to the right and proceeds between a cluster of modest houses. Hidden behind these dwellings is Clonegal Castle.

It is easy to miss the main entrance the first time you come. Set back from the street is a gateway which opens onto a majestic drive which in turn leads up through an avenue of trees. Clonegal Castle rises in the distance and presents a severe, oblong silhouette — a mix of tall windows, parapets and grey stone. Across the lawns to the left as you face the castle is a beautiful row of ancient yews, some 600 years old, and in a nearby field is the Bullawn Stone, a natural altar used for rites of healing.

Clonegal Castle is the home of the 21st Baron of Strathloch, Lawrence Durdin-Robertson, his wife Pamela, and his sister Olivia. Together, on the vernal equinox of 1976, they formed the Fellowship of Isis — a now international magical order 'dedicated to spreading the Religion of the Goddesses throughout the world'.

Inside Clonegal Castle one can easily become oblivious to the outside world. The panel-lined corridors are dark and formidable and in several of the larger rooms huge faded tapestries line the walls from floor to ceiling. In the dining room, gilt-framed ancestors peer down from their canvases while in another wing, the small conservatory is overrun by a huge, tangled grape-vine. Legend has it that the vine has grown from a cutting taken at Hampton Court so it is quite likely, as Olivia mentions enthusiastically, that Queen Elizabeth I and Nell Gwynn ate grapes from the same vine!

Baron Robertson, or Derry as he likes to be called, now describes the structure and history of the castle. He wears a blue and black tartan cap and is an impressive, if slightly austere, figure. His face is pink and smooth, his eyes clear, his speech measured. Clonegal Castle, he explains, was one of the last such buildings erected in Ireland, an authentic Jacobean castle dating from 1625. Built by the Wexford aristocrat Lord Esmonde it has been the ancestral home of the Durdin-Robertson family since 1780, and has a very colourful history. Cromwell's troops were quartered here and despoiled the battlements. The Esmondes then restored it, added much of the ornamentation and built the avenue to the village. But long before the castle was erected there was an abbey on the site, and prior to that, an ancient Druid community worshipped on the land. The sacred well used by the Druids is now incorporated within Clonegal Castle itself, and is used during the ceremonies to the Goddess.

A tour of the castle takes us down into the basement to the Temple of the Stars, a series of rooms and passage-ways housing several shrines and chapels. There are 12 such shrines — one for each sign of the Zodiac — and each has symbols and motifs of the Universal Goddess appropriate to that astrological motif. There are statues and paintings of Isis, Aphrodite, Diana, Hathor . . . the procession of images is rich and varied. Numerous female forms are presented for, as Derry says in his booklet *The Religion of the Goddess,* 'an image can be ensouled by the divinity it is intended to represent'.

The Temple of the Stars provides the setting for the ritual ordination of priests and priestesses within the Fellowship of Isis. Olivia believes that 'every human being is potentially of the Priesthood' and that it is only through an authentic mystical experience that one can 'recognize one's immortality'.

The first phase of Priesthood, says Olivia, involves obedience and service to the deity, and this is expressed through hymns of praise and the quest for salvation. The second phase is more of a visionary leap forward — identifying totally with the deity so that the person becomes a human channel for the spiritual presence. Because women are 'naturally psychic and intuitive' they are ideally suited to this type of religious expression and the Fellowship of Isis sees its role as aiding such spiritual transformation. Olivia calls the Temple 'a half-way house between the other world and this'.

In rites of ordination candidates are presented for the Priesthood and take vows to serve the Goddess and express themselves through her. Usually a sizeable group of devotees assembles for each ordination ceremony — there may be as many as 15 or 20 Fellowship members on each occasion.

Fully robed in ceremonial regalia, they enter the castle from the gardens and the yew tree avenue. The group then makes its way down the steps into the Temple of the Stars and gathers around the ancient well, which is sacred to the Irish goddess of prosperity, Brigit. Here the holy water is presented to the candidates, who drink it to enhance the psychic vision and healing in their lives. The group now moves further into the Temple to confront the Dark Mother.

A Fellowship member personifying the Celtic queen of demons, Morrigan, sits before them in the castle dungeon. She wears dark robes and a formidable and somewhat gruesome tribal mask — the idea is to present the least attractive aspect of the Goddess as a counterpoint to the beauty, love and happiness she also bestows. Here is the Goddess in her most menacing form — a hag, a potential destroyer. The candidates are asked if they fear her but, attuned to the spirit of the occasion, they offer their love and submission. Morrigan then removes her mask and reveals herself as the radiant Goddess of the Moon — a force of life and light transcending the darkness and the limitations of thought and form symbolized by the dungeon.

Moving still further into the temple, past the many shrines and chapels that similarly show different forms of the feminine, the candidates come to the high altar.

Here Olivia and Derry stand in ceremony before the multi-tiered candlesticks and a fine, ornate statue of the Universal

Goddess. Derry announces that the ordination is about to take place and seeks testimonies from those admitting the candidates to office. Offerings are now made to the Goddess and Olivia asks the new initiates which tradition they will follow. Perhaps they will dedicate themselves to Isis, or Aphrodite, or Diana — or perhaps to more localized goddesses like Dana, mother of the Tuatha de Danann, or Cesara, Banba or Fodhla. Olivia, as Priestess, now anoints the head, heart and hands of each candidate and presents them with a crown and wand. As she does so she makes a blessing over them:

'With this crown I dignify thy head, with this stole I hallow thy heart, with this wand I strengthen thy will for good ... may you be blessed by the Goddess.'

Derry now announces their acceptance into the Priesthood and the candidates make their first invocations as initiates, calling on the Goddess to enrich their lives and those about them. The ceremony ends with a symbolic 'coming forth from the womb' as members of the Fellowship of Isis proceed into the gardens once again.

Of course, not all members of the Fellowship of Isis can attend an ordination in Ireland. Olivia relates an amusing incident where the ceremony was conducted over the telephone — between Clonegal and Atlanta, Georgia. The phonebill at the Castle had not been paid and the telephone was cut off the day before the ceremony. Fortunately this shortcoming was rectified just half an hour before the ordination but arrangements also had to be made to amplify the sound-reception so both parties could hear each other across the Atlantic. Meanwhile, the members of the Fellowship had assembled fully robed at the Castle to welcome American goddess-worshipper Morgan le Fay and her friends in Atlanta to the mysteries of the Goddess.

The Americans had chosen, as their personal deities, Demeter and Persephone — the goddesses of fertility and rebirth worshipped in the rites of Eleusis in ancient Greece. Everything went to plan, and as Olivia says cheerfully, 'We had a wonderful ceremony and heard every word they said, quite clearly.'

Derry and Olivia would readily admit that they are quite eccentric but they have an endearing charm and honesty which provides the Fellowship with considerable credibility — whether one believes in the Goddess or not.

Of the two, Derry is the scholar and theologian while Olivia is more the intuitive visionary.

Derry was born in England in 1920 and grew up in Ireland from the age of five. After a stint in the Irish Army he decided to pursue a more peaceful career in the Church and studied for three years at the Wells Theological College in Somerset, just after the Second World War. After his ordination he became a parish rector at Aghold, County Wicklow, and then spent five years as rector in East Bilney, Norfolk. By now he had become interested in comparative religion and the more unorthodox realms of spiritualism, theosophy and the occult. Then, in 1966, he experienced the revelation that the feminine aspect of deity was all-important, or in other words, 'that God was female'.

This led, predictably, to problems with orthodox theology. 'Christianity, for the most part, ignores the Goddess,' says Derry, 'although in Catholicism the Virgin Mary is as close as they get. Nevertheless, they are very careful not to include her in the Trinity.'

Convinced that Christianity's claim to exclusive truth was historically vulnerable, Derry pursued his study of comparative religion with even more fervour. In an address given at the Wexford Festival in 1974, he explained to his audience that man's first religious impulses were predominantly feminine for, of the Stone-Age sculptures known to man, 55 were female and only five male.[2] The latter were poorly executed and clearly of a secondary nature — man's first religion was thus the cult of the Goddess. Derry then explained that the Goddess was universal, appearing in China as a figure of mercy, Kwan-yin, in Babylon as Ishtar, the Queen of Heaven, and in Egypt as Maat and Bast. He also pointed out that in a Biblical context, the Hebrew word for God, *Elohim*, combined the word *Eloh*, a goddess and *Im*, a plural masculine suffix, so the word would be more appropriately translated as 'deities' or 'pantheon'. As such there was no theological justification for the rigidly patriarchal emphasis of Judaism and Christianity.

Derry also noted that the Hebrew word for the Holy Spirit, *Ruach*, was usually considered feminine, and that during the Greek and Roman occupations of Palestine the Holy Ghost was similarly regarded as female. So the idea of God as a bearded ruler on a throne was quite clearly of limited application.

Derry now believes that what is emerging in western culture — whether through the growth of feminism as a sociopolitical force or through paganism as a spiritual expression — is a return to the cult of the Goddess. He also equates this revival with a return to the psychic and intuitive qualities traditionally associated with woman rather than with man. Expressing this as a reaction against Christianity Derry explains:

'The upsurge in the occult comes from within. It cannot find containment in the existing western religions so it has to find expression in some other form. The old religions, and paga-

Rosaleen Norton surrounded by her occult
paraphernalia

'Lucifer' by Rosaleen Norton, from the 1949
exhibition

Janet and Stewart Farrar, working 'sky clad' in a ritual

The regal setting of Clonegal Castle

Participants in an initiation
ceremony at Clonegal Castle
Derry is in the centre

A goddess shrine at Clonegal

Morrigan – the celtic queen of
demons. This mask is used in
ritual ceremonies in Clonegal
Castle

Alex Sanders in his mask: the 'Aztec' takes
possession

Alex Sanders' Book of Shadows

The black god Ghede, or Guede,
voodoo Lord of Life and Death
Painting by Michael Bertiaux

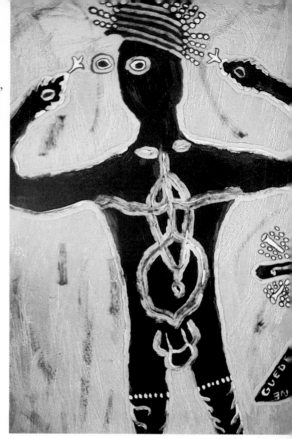

Voodoo magician Michael Bertiaux at his altar

Michael Aquino, head of the
Temple of Set, with Lilith Sinclair

The Temple of Set in San
Francisco is one of several occult
orders that have revived the
ancient Egyptian pantheon. Set is
shown seated, on the right

A stone circle used by the Wiccans of Circle Sanctuary

Jim Alan and Selena Fox from
Circle Sancturary

Z. Budapest and friends in Berkeley, California

Swiss fantasy artist H. R. Giger at home — amidst the dark thought-forms of his mind

nism if you like to call it that, make far more allowance for
spiritualism and the occult than orthodox Christianity, which
is basically patriarchal. The patriarchal religions have a certain fixed framework and their followers must believe within
those limits ... they don't allow for spontaneous inspiration or
revelation.'

Olivia, like Derry, is very much in favour of the development of spiritual consciousness and encourages members of
the Fellowship to stimulate their psychic faculties as far as
possible. Her own experiences have been both awesome and
bizarre.

Once, she had a very particular vision of the Goddess Dana
as a being of 'crystallized white light'. The Goddess appeared
to her in full consciousness in the middle of the night and
seemed to communicate through telepathic power. Olivia
recalls the experience quite vividly:

'She had long, golden, wavy hair and a most beautiful face.
She was wearing a turquoise blue coat embroidered with gold
that mingled with her hair rather strangely. I was filled with
the most wonderful ecstasy and happiness.' The Goddess then
rose up and ascended into the sky.

Olivia says that, for her, the experience was 'real' and makes
the point that profound psychic experiences don't happen to
her very often. However, she is convinced that the being she
saw is accessible to others and is possibly the same as the
Blessed Lady who appeared in the so-called Miracle of Fatima
in 1917, at Lourdes, and at the village of Knock in County
Mayo. In the last instance, an entire community experienced
a vision of a woman in a blue robe, accompanied by Joseph and
John, and there is now a Roman Catholic basilica on this
sacred ground. Olivia interprets the phenomenon somewhat
differently though. Perhaps both the Virgin Mary and Dana

are one and the same being: the spiritual Queen of Ireland.

On a more practical level, Olivia conducts meditations which encourage Fellowship members to tap the spiritual aspects of consciousness. These 'astral journeys' are really exercises in developing the imagination and are held in the Temple of the Stars. Once, at a Fellowship gathering, a tinker-woman came to the castle and said to Olivia in her broad Irish accent: 'Hey mum, where's the magic carpet? I've heard the people here all sit on it and go off on a grand journey.' At first Olivia didn't understand what she meant but then she realized that word had got around in the village about the 'astral journey' meetings at the castle. The unusual spiritual practices at Clonegal were fast becoming part of local folklore!

Olivia has described several of her own visionary experiences in her book *The Call of Isis* and, like Derry, she is a prolific writer. Her recent works, like *Rite of Rebirth* and *Urania: Ceremonial Magic of the Goddess* deal primarily with ritual procedures in the Temple but her earlier writings were published internationally. Olivia studied at the National University in Dublin and as a left-wing pacifist became intensely interested in social welfare and the problems of the under-privileged. Her book on Anglo-Irish life, *Field of the Stranger* was published both in Britain and the United States in 1948 and became a best-seller, and she followed it with other works like *It's an Old Irish Custom* and *Dublin Phoenix*. However her direction after the war was increasingly towards things spiritual and she found the inner world now much more real than her external, secular environment. Most people, she feels, still live rather empty lives and the awakening of mythic consciousness can add a valuable new dimension. However she is adamant that the ceremonies in the Temple are in no way intended to be escapist. In the act of ordination, for example, the emphasis is on enhancing one's life through the Goddess: 'You don't despise what you've got,' says Olivia. 'You're not starting again, you're offering what you have in accepting deity.'

An important aspect of the Fellowship of Isis is that it transcends denominational boundaries. Catholics, Protestants, Buddhists, Hindus, Moslems, neopagans — all are welcome and many come regularly. Others communicate by letter, sharing rituals and broadening their range of contacts via the Isis newsletter.

The present membership stands at over 5000, with representatives from over 53 countries, including Britain, the United States, Canada, Australia and several nations in Europe. However around half the members are from western Africa, especially Nigeria, Ghana and the Ivory Coast. Derry feels the traditional African religious beliefs are quite compatible with the aims of the Fellowship since both, at heart, are polytheistic, or multi-dimensional. The rites at Clonegal Castle thus provide a framework for developing old religious ideas in a modern western context, and bringing diverse peoples together.

It is hard bringing oneself to leave the castle for its appeal as a spiritual centre is enormous. The road from Bunclody and Clonegal leads north through Tullow and Baltinglass to the southern suburbs of Dublin. Here, on the outskirts of the city, row after row of mean grey houses peer forth at passers-by and life resumes a more pedestrian quality. In these streets the ordinariness of everyday life reasserts itself and the magic of Clonegal Castle seems distant and of another era. It is as if we have come through a time-warp and entered another, very much less enchanted, dimension.

And yet, as Olivia herself would say, there is a message in

this perception. The essential task is to awaken the Goddess in the everyday world, attune ourselves once again to the patterns of Nature. Even in the context of the city it is our task to find her.

Something of this sort has in fact happened with the goddess-oriented magical group in Perth called the Temple of the Mother. Like the Fellowship of Isis it acknowledges the universal aspects of the White Goddess, while paying special homage to the mysteries of ancient Egypt.

Heading the Temple is Levanah — a dark-haired, olive-skinned woman with striking features and a meticulous, systematic approach to her daily affairs. A business-woman with special skills in administration, Levanah helped run a large civil engineering enterprise in her native New Zealand before coming to Perth. She applies very much the same sort of efficient management to the Temple of the Mother.

Levanah is of German and Maori extraction but her spiritual home is in Egypt. She was raised as a Roman Catholic but feels she has lived past lives in the Bast temples of the Nile Delta, and in Nubia where she marched in processions to the Temple of Philae. However it was some time before these impressions welled up inside her.

Levanah recalls that when she was about six years old her father would take her away from the convent in Wanganui on weekends, and they would spend time together watching the full moon. Levanah felt even then that the Moon was a 'sacred being' and she wondered in her innocent way if it were somehow connected with the Virgin Mary and the Holy Ghost — it was certainly awesome to behold.

At the age of 16 Levanah joined the Rosicrucians and found she had 'strong prophetic qualities, even then' but she was still a devout Roman Catholic and was attending Mass every morning.

Then, after a period of overseas travel, she immersed herself in politics for five years — specializing in publicity for the National Party, a group aligned with conservatism and free enterprise in New Zealand. Later her businesses started to expand also. By this time married, she had 80 employees in the civil engineering firm she had developed with her husband, and was running a fashionable beauty salon as well. Things for a time were booming and Levanah became very wealthy — but then came the crunch.

For no obvious reason engineering in New Zealand went into a dramatic decline and Levanah and her husband lost a lot of money. It was time for a new start.

Levanah came over to Perth, liked what she saw, and decided to stay. However the most dramatic change came when Levanah visited Egypt.

It was here that she met the 'spiritual master' who was to change her life. He was a practising Moslem and worked in a mosque in Heliopolis, but he also had a deep and special link with ancient Egypt. It was through him that Levanah became attuned with Isis, the Mother Goddess. It was through him that she discovered Egypt 'had her heart'.

'We spent many, many days in the desert together,' she recalls, 'and as he spoke to me I realized he was describing a system that I had within me — that he was awakening my ancient self. As a person he was very, very beautiful. He radiated much love and light and his teachings often came like a vibration from within him — it was almost like clairvoyant pictures before my eyes, an unveiling of knowledge...'

Levanah returned to Perth eager to put the Egyptian mysteries into practice. She had already met Peter Barwick —

an Alexandrian witch who was running The Magic Circle bookshop in Perth — and with him had explored more traditional patterns of witchcraft. But now there was an opportunity for a completely different religious expression, and one which for her drew on deep levels of mythic awareness.

Details of appropriate rituals came flooding into her mind and she began writing them down. All the old words, the ancient prayers, and the well-loved songs were returning. The Goddess was stirring within her.

It was clear that Peter would be her magical partner in the new work, although he had come from a different tradition and would have to adapt. Always buried in books as a child, Peter had a love of ancient and spiritual things and was drawn originally to books on ancient Rome, to Lobsang Rampa's works on Tibetan mysticism, to spiritualism, and to the Jehovah's Witnesses. But none of these seemed right for him and as a teenager he continued his private quest — 'always seeking'.

Around the age of 17 he first came into contact with writings on witchcraft by the occultist Paul Huson and then, a few years later, he joined a coven and was initiated as a witch. He was working in the bookshop and giving lectures on the Tarot and the Kabbalah when he first met Levanah.

The change from witchcraft to the Egyptian mysteries made a strong impact on him. He says now that the only way of attaining personal freedom is by realizing we are part of life. And the Egyptian rites helped him to broaden his vision. In particular, Levanah showed him that he could draw on the *neters* — the ancient Egyptian gods or life-energies — and enhance his very being through them.

'Our aim,' says Peter, in explaining his present approach,

'is to contact the *neters* so that we may mirror them in our everyday actions. This means we can be a better father, or a better mother, or a better priest — whatever it is — and manifest the *neters* more purely in our everyday lives. What I get from magic and working with the Temple of the Mother and Levanah, is to realize the joyousness of life, that life is free-flowing and a very, very precious thing.'

There are 40 members in the outer order of the Temple and 13 in the inner circle. Many of the members have belonged formerly to witchcraft covens or have explored a variety of other esoteric traditions. They come to the Temple to learn authentic Egyptian invocations, to perform the ancient songs and dances and to relive the old ways. They wear carefully tailored Egyptian costumes, they make their own implements, and they perform their ceremonies impeccably. This is the way Levanah has taught them. And the Yanchep caves, north-west of the city, are a favourite spot for performing magic.

Yanchep lies on a coastal plain of yellow, sandy soil. The earth is still rich in iron but the lime has been leached and redeposited — cementing the sand into limestone. Deep beneath the earth are a number of cave systems containing caverns, streams, and crystalline pools with mirror-still reflections. Here stalactites grow at the rate of one inch every hundred years, and the largest caverns have long and exquisite tentacles of glistening limestone which reach down from the ceilings in an ornate display.

Tonight members of the Temple have come to the caves beneath a radiant full moon that casts a bright grey light across the landscape. It is a long and arduous trek down into the caves with all the ritual equipment, the flowers of celebration, and the ornamental hangings, but in due course it is done, and the ceremony can get underway.

Candlelight flickers across the copper-hewn face of Nefertiti, a masked drummer stands poised ready to beat a compelling rhythm on his drum, and in the foreground — at the edge of a large pool — is a cauldron bearing an Egyptian ankh. The group members now come forward in procession as the ceremony begins. The group moves anti-clockwise into a circle and all subsequent formations of this kind are in the same direction — following the sun.

There are dances and chants hailing Isis, Osiris, Nepthys and Anubis, invocations to the Great Mother Isis in the East, and more mantric songs in praise of the ancient gods.

Now Levanah steps into the crystal water alone. She is garbed in a long black robe and walks in a dignified but serene way to the centre of the pool. There are further invocations now, for Levanah has become possessed by the spirit of Isis and the praises are intense and more powerful still.

Soon she is joined, in turn, by one devotee after another as each in turn wades forth into the pool, throwing brightly coloured flowers in praise of the Great Goddess. Finally everyone surrounds her, and Isis is amongst them all — a presence from ancient times, alive once again like a song in their hearts.

For Peter the rites of Isis show a way back to a more sensitive and caring lifestyle, a way that many of us have forgotten.

'I feel the Goddess is very important,' he says, 'because man has lost touch with his feelings. We live in an age of reason where feeling and loving and dancing and flowing have been lost. The Temple of the Mother, and the Goddess, give me ways of achieving these feeling states, and I think the earth needs mothering as well. It's been brutalized and damaged, and the mother-force has been lost in our society.'

Magic, like poetry and song, has brought a new dimension into his life, a new way of perceiving that adds a richness not present before:

'Magic has helped me improve my life by making me more aware, more aware of my own self. This means I can grow as a human being, and become more aware of my environment — flow within it more freely and more fruitfully, and with more meaning.'

Levanah feels much the same way — a sense of privilege in drawing down the energies of Isis on behalf of her group:

'Magic gives me vitality. It feeds me. It makes me constantly aware of change. It makes me constantly aware that I'm part of this universe and everybody else is part of it too ... I actually *do feel* like I am the Great Mother. I feel like I am the earth, I'm sea, I'm everything feminine. And the priest and priestesses before me — as I look into their eyes and they look into my eyes, there is a most incredible openness that one doesn't find in the mundane world. We can only experience that within the sacredness of a ritual where we have worked to invoke the *neters* within ourselves, opening ourselves to the learning. And as they kneel in front of me during the full moon, I have this feeling of being dissolved and being part of them, and of them being part of me, and of everything dissolving, all of Nature, everything dissolving around us, all of us becoming one.'

So it is that the ancient Goddess can still touch modern lives, that in a deeply felt way she is once again reaching her followers through the call of Nature. It is a call to respect the sanctity of the earth, and a call to recover a feminine quality that modern man has neglected.

Not all magicians, however, hear this call — or even wish to heed it. And some go to great lengths to actually avoid it.

Indeed there are some occultists whose paths in the mysteries have taken them to quite different regions of the mind and of Nature — into the dark side of Voodoo magic and among the cults of the shadow.

1. Cheri Lesh, 'Goddess Worship; the Subversive Religion', *Twelve Together*, Los Angeles, May 1975.

2. Derry obtained this information from Erich Neumann's book, *The Great Mother*, London 1954, p.95.

CHAPTER 4

From Voodoo to the Temple of Set

High up, on the thirty-third floor of a residential apartment block on South Michigan Avenue, Chicago, lives a Voodoo priest. He is a gently spoken man with intense eyes, heavy-rimmed glasses and a dark, full-bodied beard. By day he works as a government counsellor, hearing welfare grievances mainly from the Haitian community in the city. In his private time, however, he celebrates the mysteries of Guede and Legbha, the Voodoo counterpart of the dead and risen Christ.

Michael Bertiaux is by no means a typical occultist. Indeed it is difficult to say whether — in the traditional sense — he is a black or white magician. He's not really sure himself. Most occultists, he says, resort to techniques at both ends of the spectrum. However he does admit that 'life is so complex that we sometimes have to do things to survive that would have been considered, at one time, forms of black magic.'

Bertiaux, like many occultists, is a Capricorn, and also has a Neptune ascendant. Born in Seattle on 18 January 1935, he grew up in a family that was primarily Theosophical. His father tended towards Zen Buddhism, while his mother was interested in spiritualism and the development of psychic powers. The Bertiaux ancestry was a combination of English, French and Irish.

Like a number of ceremonial magicians, Bertiaux's career began within the ranks of orthodox religion and then departed for the fringe. Educated initially by Jesuit fathers, he later attended an Anglican seminary in order to train for a career in the Church. He graduated with honours, was ordained, and became curate of an Anglican parish in West Seattle. It was shortly after this that his career took an oblique turn towards the occult.

An opportunity arose for Michael Bertiaux to teach philosophy in the Anglican church college in Port-au-Prince, Haiti. He decided to go, and as part of his training in 'culture shock' transitions, studied with the distinguished anthropologist Margaret Mead.

The first visit to Haiti was only for three months but some interesting contacts were made. These included traditional Voodoo practitioners with French esoteric leanings who were keen to see their system of Haitian magic adapted for an American audience. They introduced Bertiaux to the key concepts and asked him to help them present the more positive side of Voodoo which, so far, had not been available in the West. Bertiaux was intrigued and promised to stay in touch. He returned to Seattle, maintained contact with the *vouduns* from Haiti, and began to see that his spiritual path was changing direction. It was becoming increasingly clear to him that he would have to leave the Anglican church to join the Haitian mystery tradition.

The French occult connection in Haiti derives from two eighteenth-century mystics, Louis Claude de Saint-Martin and Martinez de Pasqually. The latter was a Rosicrucian disciple of Emanuel Swedenborg, and the founder of an occult group called the Order of the Elect Cohens. He was inspired by Gnosticism and the Kabbalah, and believed that one could only gain spiritual salvation by contacting the Divine Source of All Being, and by participating in an initiation ceremony to invoke one's Holy Guardian Angel. Saint-Martin joined de Pasqually's order in 1768 and after the leader's death in 1774 became the dominant figure in the group. Collectively they became known as Martinists. There were Martinist orders in several different regions of France: in Foix, Bordeaux, Paris and Lyons — and by the end of the eighteenth century, also in Haiti. However here the tradition tended to blend with Voodoo.

After a period in abeyance, Martinism revived in Haiti in the 1890s and between the two world wars the so-called Neo-Pythagorean Gnostic Church came into being. This church advocates the invocation of angels and planetary spirits, is highly ritualistic, and regards the Eucharist as the central initiation. Members of the clergy claim to be clairvoyant, often have visions during the Mass, and speak in a mystical language which — as Michael Bertiaux later explained — is a type of 'Slavonic Voodoo', resembling the Pentecostal speaking-in-tongues.

The present head and supreme hierophant of the Gnostic Church in Haiti is Dr Hector Jeane Maine. Born in Haiti and educated in France, Dr Jean Maine was initiated by a Martinist bishop and now lives in the mountains near Leogane. Michael Bertiaux's role within the Church is to be its representative for all Caucasian-American members. He was formally initiated into the Gnostic–Voodoo mysteries on 15 August 1963.

The following year he resigned from the Anglican Church and moved to Wheaton, Illinois, where he worked as a researcher for the Theosophical Society. This brought him into contact with several prominent Liberal Catholics, including Dr Henry Smith, Bishop Stephan Hoeller and Bishop Gregory, who was also a key figure in the Russian Orthodox Church. Liberal Catholicism maintains a high degree of ceremonial, and appeals to many mystically inclined Theosophists. Its influence has left its mark on Bertiaux to the extent that in his ceremonial workings he could easily be mistaken for an Eastern Orthodox priest. However it becomes apparent that the forces he is invoking lie well outside the range of mainstream Christian beliefs.

In the late 1960s Michael Bertiaux began to swing back more heavily into the Voodoo tradition. Several Haitian *vouduns* had moved to suburban Evanston — there was a sizeable Haitian community in Chicago at that time — and Bertiaux was consecrated as an adept within an organization known as the Monastery of the Seven Rays. Bertiaux considers this occult order to be the 'magical offshoot of Roman Catholicism' although it is rather less likely that the Vatican would consider it so.

Certainly, the role of the dead and risen Christ remains central to the cosmology, but the spiritual atmosphere is quite different from that in Christianity. There is a strong input from Voodoo — a central magical technique is to transform one's consciousness into that of an 'astral tarantula', and one's occult powers are obtained from Voodoo spirits of possession known as *loas*. A far cry, indeed, from the orthodox scriptures.

The Monastery's cosmology — or map of higher consciousness — resembles the Kabbalistic Tree of Life except that the Hebrew god-names are replaced by their Voodoo counterparts. In Bertiaux's magical ceremonies — which feature monotone chanting, specific ritual gestures made with the fingers, and the extensive use of implements like the censer, bell and magic crystal — most of the real work is done on the inner planes. The key to working magic, says Bertiaux, is the development of powers of visualization.

On the walls of Bertiaux's apartment hang numerous oil paintings of Voodoo gods, and these are used as an aid to stimulate the imagination, to summon the Spirit from what he calls the 'ocean of the unconscious'. Among these works, which Bertiaux painted himself in a primitive, atavistic Haitian style, are representations of the Voodoo witch-goddess Maconda, 'a powerful and stabilizing influence in ritual'; the Voodoo god of lakes and rivers, who confers telepathy on his devotees; and the crucified Guede, god of the dead. The latter, says Bertiaux, is associated with Christ as the resurrected saviour, but also demonstrates that 'while the body may die, the spirit comes back many times, taking on a physical embodiment and resurrecting itself continuously through a cycle of reincarnations...'

But it is Bertiaux's concept of the astral tarantula and the idea of the temple as a magical space-ship that are the most extraordinary of all.

One of the techniques advocated in the Monastery of the Seven Rays is to visualize oneself surrounded by creatures so horrible that they ward off magical attacks from the hostile possessing entities of inner space. As the magician energizes himself in ritual, or during his meditations at night, he begins to attract what Bertiaux calls 'negative vampires' — the spirits of the dead. It is vital, he says, that one should appear strong and impregnable on the astral planes — and it is for this reason that he has to imaginatively extend the magical circle in his temple into a strong psychic sphere, guarded at the eight points by different Voodoo *loas.* Meanwhile the magician transforms in the astral imagination into a were-tarantula and prepares to direct his space-ship to different regions of the inner cosmic terrain. As a 'spider-sorcerer' or 'spider-magician', writes Bertiaux in one of his order papers, 'you have woven your web by meeting with your own magical force each of the eight sources of cosmic energy. Thus, cosmic energy is met by god-energy...'

Bertiaux explains this further within the broad context of Voodoo ritual:

'Every time we do a ceremony we participate somehow in the god consciousness, or the energy behind the ceremony. I think it is a form of possession without a doubt, and represents the way in which the gods manifest themselves in human experience...

'Voodoo and Gnosticism both work with the number eight because it is a significant power zone. In Voodoo it is represented by the mystical symbolism of the spider of space, the space deity. It represents the way in which the mind of the priest makes contact with all the possibilities of the world of space and time. For the magician to achieve a certain state of power he *becomes* that being in order to mediumistically receive the powers from the god behind the animal form.'

So how does the temple actually become a 'space-ship' and how does the spider-magician function within it?

'The temple is a space-ship because it is a way of moving through the different spaces of consciousness. In fact the gestures of the ritual are designed to build a spherical vehicle for the priest's activities in other worlds. The priest is a spider because what he is doing is actually bringing into his own life the experience of other worlds, and then he's joining himself through the web of his consciousness, to all the different parts of the spiritual experience.

'Every time he does something — a gesture, a word, a movement with some object — he is, in a sense, making contact between his web and something outside it. What he is doing is connecting himself to those worlds and dimensions.'

However, in the particular forms of Voodoo practised by members of the Monastery, there is also something of a magical trade-off. As the order papers make clear, some spirit-entities are allowed to penetrate the protective web and draw on the magician's life-force in return for providing specific occult powers that are desired. Summoned as the magician arouses himself erotically, the spirits 'come down upon his body' draining the vitality of the mind and replacing it with psychic power. It is a method fraught with dangers for it is the very epitome of spirit-possession and leaves the occultist — at the moment of mental surrender — open to all manner of occult forces. As Bertiaux warns his students: 'Does this occult exchange provide sufficient compensation for the man who must sacrifice himself to nocturnal appetites of the most perverse type?'

Presumably, in his own case, the risks have proven worthwhile. Also known to order members as Michael Aquarius, Bertiaux is now one of the chief adepts of the Monastery of the Seven Rays and has been largely responsible for disseminating its mysteries by mail to correspondents around the world. And although Voodoo magic clearly has its dark side, Bertiaux believes that a substantial part of what he does ritually has a positive side too. The invocation performed before us in the temple is intended, he says, 'to distribute force'. It is '... a healing intended generally for the whole face of the earth, for all humanity, and for all those beings in need of some kind of spiritual strength.

'What we are doing in our rituals is describing what is going on in the spiritual world,' — portraying and summoning the spirits through gestures, magical implements and ceremonial regalia.

There is no doubt that in his dramatic red and gold robe Michael Bertiaux presents an imposing form. Seated on a chair beside his paintings of Voodoo spirits, he has a regal air — a high priest serving exotic gods before an even stranger altar.

Yet it is this sense of ceremonial grandeur which makes one pause and take stock, just for a moment. Many storeys below us, in the streets of Chicago, up-tight taxi drivers and frenzied commuters bustle about their daily routines unaware that strange spirits move among them.

In a quiet residential street in Zurich something of a comparable nature is taking place inside the house of fantasy artist, H. R. Giger. Giger is best known for his dramatic visual effects in the science-fiction film *Alien*, and for the haunting, nightmarish paintings which have been reproduced in his books *Necronomicon* and *N.Y. City*. Like Michael Bertiaux, Giger too is quietly spoken, gentle, and even shy — but from within his mind a torrent of dark images surges forth to be released onto canvas. Visiting Giger's house, and seeing the large surreal panels which adorn its walls, is like experiencing an exorcism.

Giger says that he does not understand the processes which underly his painting but that he makes use, essentially, of the mediumistic or 'automatic' style adopted by several surrealists, including Max Ernst, Oscar Dominguez and Wolfgang Paalen. Giger maintains that he opens the door to his unconscious mind by confronting a blank canvas and suspending conscious thought. Then, as the spontaneous images start to build before his eyes, he adds details and texture with his airbrush. He says he likes the airbrush because of its 'tremendous directness'.

'It enables me to project my visions directly onto the pictorial surface, freezing them immediately.'

There is no doubt that, in terms of his art, Giger is very much a magician — conjuring dramatic visionary compositions which take us straight into the darker recesses of human consciousness. His paintings have been praised by the distinguished surrealists Ernst Fuchs and Salvador Dali, and he has been called a genius by psychedelic researchers Timothy Leary and Stanislav Grof. And his work, unquestionably, has an authentic magical calibre rarely seen in modern art, which links him in spirit with such tortured masters of the visionary perspective as Hieronymus Bosch and Lucas Cranach.

Giger lives an unobtrusive existence in a double-storey terrace house just a few minutes drive from Zurich's busy international airport. His living room downstairs is dominated by the remarkable paintings which first earned him international recognition, and which feature Medusa-like women with ghostly-pale skin, snakes in their hair and strange shapes and forms writhing around them. Claws, needles, machine-guns and barbs also feature strongly, and, for most people, his works are distinctly disturbing — yet fascinating at the same time. They also have an extraordinary three-dimensional quality which lifts them beyond the plane of the wall so that they become part of the living ambience of the room.

In the centre of the long table which occupies his living room is an engraved pentagram, and also candlesticks whose flames cast an eerie light on the paintings nearby. A tall row of shelves in one corner of the room reveals a row of skulls and authentic shrunken heads from a cannibal tribe. It is here that Giger has placed his Oscar won for *Alien* — a tribute to his bizarre imagination.

Upstairs Giger has his studio. At one end it is total chaos — a litter of splattered paint, brushes and discarded works of art. Here he experiments with his airbrush techniques, spraying patterns through metal grids and exploring different textures of light and shade.

At the other end of the long, open room, is a large black table with bulbous legs and an extraordinary mirror sheen on its pristine surface. Fashioned substantially from a heavy moulded plastic, it is accompanied by several tall chairs surmounted with skulls and shaped to give the impression of distorted vertebrae. An ashen-grey version of these chairs — seemingly fashioned from bone itself — has pride of place at the head of the table. And gracing the long wall above, is another large panel — this time depicting a horned devil, a silver pentagram and dark, hostile serpents.

Giger has little real explanation for these remarkable manifestations. 'I try to come close to my imagination,' he says in his broken English, 'I have something in my head and I try to work it out — like a kind of exorcism...' Giger recognizes the adverse effect his work has on many of the people who see it — including his respectable and conservative mother — but he is keen to point out that if his work seems dark, he is not this way himself.

'My childhood was very happy,' he says almost apologetically, 'and my parents have been very nice to me.' He ponders a while and then adds: 'I think most of the images in my paintings *are* evil, but you can't say that *I'm* evil. It's just that evil is much, much more interesting than paradise...'

Giger was born in 1940 in the small Swiss town of Chur, an 'unbearable' place of 'high mountains...and petty bourgeois attitudes'. Growing up there, he had nightmares in his parents' house and would imagine 'gigantic bottomless shafts bathing in a pale yellow light'. In his *Necronomicon* he writes that, 'On the walls, steep and treacherous wooden stairways without bannisters led down into the yawning abyss' and the cellar in the house gave rise to the image of 'a monstrous labyrinth, where all kinds of dangers lay in wait for me'. This feeling is certainly conveyed in his paintings for, time and again, the figures seemed trapped and tormented in gruesome, tortuous tunnels and there is no apparent path of escape.

As a child, Giger built skeletons of cardboard, wire and plaster, and he recalls that he also had an 'overwhelming disgust of worms and snakes' — a loathing which still manifests itself in his paintings today. He also had a fascination for pistols and guns of all sorts, and during his military service was accidentally nearly shot on more than one occasion.

If Giger is haunted by images from his past this is quite understandable, for there have been many crises in his life. One of the most traumatic involved the beautiful actress, Li Tobler.

Giger met Li in 1966 when she was 18 and living with another man. However Giger moved into her attic apartment and in due course they became lovers. Giger recalls that Li 'had enormous vitality and a great appetite for life'. She also wanted her life to be 'short but intense'.

Li is the prototype for the many ethereal women in his paintings who peer forth from the torment of snakes, needles, and stifling bone prisons — to a world beyond. Giger painted Li's body several times with an airbrush and there are several photographs of her posing naked — like a woman of mystery struggling to emerge from a nightmare that has possessed her soul.

Around this time Giger inherited his present house as a legacy from his uncle, and Li moved in. But the idyll, says Giger, 'was all too short'. Li had a hectic schedule for her theatrical performances around the country, was irresistibly drawn to numerous other lovers, and was beginning to experience the pressures of life in the fast lane. On Whit Monday 1975 she shot herself with a revolver.

It may be too simplistic to say that Li haunts Giger still, for his life is full of beautiful and exotic women who are fascinated by his art and by his bohemian lifestyle. But there is no doubting that the simultaneous agony and joy of life with Li Tobler established the dynamic of fear and transcendence which is present in many of his paintings.

Giger maintains that although he has studied the occult works of Aleister Crowley, he is not a magician in the orthodox sense for he does not perform rituals, engage in invocations, or summon spirits. But one could hardly find a better temple of the black arts than Giger's main living room, and the beings which inhabit his paintings are themselves like a pantheon of demons. For Giger, in a very real way, makes magic spontaneously. When the thin veil across his psyche is drawn aside just a little, remarkable and tempestuous visions come forth. It is as if the dark gods are emerging once again from the nightmares of his past.

Elsewhere even darker forces are afoot, although the systematic pursuit of Satanism seems still to be a comparatively rare phenomenon — at least in terms of visible occult practices in the world today. In the United States, as elsewhere, the lure of dark, exotic powers is always present in the occult, as the magician wrestles with the chaotic and often tormenting energies of the unconscious mind. The Temple of Set in San Francisco, however, provides a quite different, and much more intellectual approach to classical Satanism.

Michael Aquino, Ippsissimus and Director of the Temple of Set is far removed from one's image of a typical Satanist. He doesn't defile crucifixes, indulge in human sacrifices, participate in magical attacks against Christians or sign pacts of blood with the Devil. He has a doctorate in political science, maintains a high-ranking position in government administration and even has a sense of humour — his iridescent brown Lincoln Continental sports a number plate which reads, simply, 'I'd rather do magic'.

At 39 years of age, Aquino has a fresh complexion and a thoroughly professional demeanour although his tufted eyebrows and carefully styled widow's peak are at times disconcerting. He is undoubtedly a thoughtful and intelligent man and, indeed, several aspects of his philosophy are reminiscent of Mahayana Buddhism and certain personal growth therapies within the Human Potential movement. So, why Satanism?

Michael Aquino came to it almost by accident. In 1968 he was in the process of graduating from the University of California at Santa Barbara and was deeply interested in the study of comparative religion and philosophy. He had explored Eastern mysticism and also existentialism, found them either incomplete or unsatisfactory, and was now — in his own words — 'a floating agnostic'.

It was in June of that year, while visiting San Francisco, that he learned that the horror film *Rosemary's Baby* was premiering in North Beach. It seemed a good idea to check it out so he went along for the opening. Then, as he was leaving the theatre, there was quite a commotion in the crowd as a black hearse drove up at the kerb-side. Several figures garbed in black robes and hoods emerged from the hearse and filed into the lobby with considerable pomp and ceremony. Heading the procession was an 'imposing gentleman with a shaven head and a Fu Manchu-style goatee' and Aquino asked who he was. He was told that it was Anton Szandor La Vey.

Aquino was unaware at the time that La Vey was head of the Church of Satan — an organization which had been established in San Francisco two years earlier. Aquino didn't make his acquaintance on that occasion but returned to San Francisco a year later. This time he visited La Vey's residence in California Street to attend some lectures on occultism and metaphysics. The mood was informal and relaxed and the lectures mostly light-hearted. One of the topics was fortune-telling with tea-leaves and crystal balls. But Aquino was impressed by the man himself. 'Underneath his somewhat mardi gras exterior,' Aquino recalls, 'I sensed an individual who did in fact have a new perspective on the human equation.'

La Vey was indeed both a showman and a serious occultist. A former lion-trainer and carnival performer, he had assisted with hypnotism displays and played in the San Francisco Ballet Orchestra. He was now working as a photographer with the police. One of his other interests was collecting books on occultism and 'obscure facets of human nature'. Convinced that most occult organizations lacked sophistication he established 'midnight magic seminars' in the early 1960s, and by 1965 was running a regular 'magic circle'.

On Walpurgisnacht 1966 he founded the Church of Satan with regular meetings each Friday night for group workings of 'Greater Black Magic'. These meetings had one specific and overriding aim — to demonstrate to participants that they could rid themselves of the 'moral hypocrisy' and guilt engendered by the mainstream religions and indulge themselves totally in pleasurable self-gratification. For a time the Church in California Street attracted considerable attention in the media — gaining a reputation as a place where ritual magicians would gather around a naked woman serving as a 'human altar' during the ceremony of the Black Mass. There were also invocations to such nefarious beings as Lucifer, Belial and Leviathan, and Satanic hymns accompanied by electric organ.

Predictably there was public outrage and condemnation from many quarters for it seemed to many that the Devil of lust and carnal desire had now incarnated in the suburbs. There were also dramatic exaggerations of Church membership — estimates as high as '50,000 card-carrying Satanists' with 'millions of sympathetic non-members waiting in the wings'.[1] But the reality, says Michael Aquino, was quite different. According to official Church records to which he had access, the initial San Francisco membership was only around 50, climbing to a nation-wide peak of 300 by 1975.

La Vey, nevertheless, attracted national attention when he published *The Satanic Bible* as a mass market paperback in 1970. Here Satan and the entire demonic hierarchy were portrayed as metaphors for hedonistic self-indulgence. The book also included rituals for invoking Satan, cursing opponents and heightening one's powers of erotic sexuality. Following the increase in public interest, however, La Vey and his wife Diane began to find it tiresome to hold meetings solely in their home, so they decided to sponsor other branches of the Church — in San Francisco and in other towns and cities across the nation. 'Grottos' were established as far afield as Louisville, Kentucky; Santa Cruz; San Jose; Los Angeles; Denver; Dayton, Ohio; Detroit; Washington D.C., and New York — mostly centred around charismatic individuals intent on spreading the word. Anton was now calling himself the High Priest of Satan, or Magus of the Age of Satan, and had established five initiatory degrees: Satanist 1°; Witch or Warlock II°; Priest or Priestess of Mendes III°; Magister IV° and Magus V°. Aquino, meanwhile, had joined the church in 1969, attaining the second degree in 1970. By the following year he was not only a grade four Satanist but editor of the Church's newsletter, *The Cloven Hoof.*

And yet all was not well with the Church of Satan. As Aquino notes in his *Crystal Tablet of Set*, the Church was starting to attract far too many 'fad-followers, egomaniacs and assorted oddballs whose primary interest in becoming Satanists was to flash their membership cards for cocktail-party notoreity'.[2] More to the point, La Vey was finding that he couldn't survive as a full-time magician on the ten dollar annual fee levied for church membership, and it was this realization which was to bring about a crisis.

In early 1975, La Vey sent out advice in the Church newsletter advising that, forthwith, all higher degrees of initiation would be available for contributions in cash, real estate or valuable objects of art. The effect, says Aquino, was shattering:

'If there had been a single unifying factor that had brought us to Satanism,' he recalls, 'it was the Church's stand against hypocrisy. So when we learned of this policy, our reaction to it was that Anton La Vey was betraying his office, betraying everything that he had worked for, for so many years.'

However there was no way of firing the leader — the

Church of Satan to all intents and purposes was vested in him. The only alternative was for the priesthood to leave.

In June 1975 an act of mass desertion took place. Key members of the priesthood across the country resigned from the Church of Satan, at the same time making it clear that they were not leaving the priesthood itself.

'In fact,' says Aquino, 'we had a sacred responsibility to take it with us.'

The result was to be the formation of a completely new church with Aquino as its leader, and the emergence of a new type of rational and intellectual Satanism. The organization would even have a new name — the Temple of Set — and a completely different orientation.

As a priest of the fourth degree Michael Aquino was the senior member of the splinter group but it was clear that new guidelines were now required from Satan himself. On the evening of 21 June 1975, in a ritual magic ceremony, Aquino summoned the Prince of Darkness himself, 'to tell us what we may do to continue our Quest'. The result, Aquino recalls, was an act of 'automatic writing...a communication from a god to a human being'. Satan now revealed himself as the ancient Egyptian god Set and named Michael Aquino as La Vey's successor. Furthermore, Aquino was described in the script as the successor to Aleister Crowley and Magus, fifth degree, of the new Aeon of Set. Gone were all references to the Christian Devil, and the *Book of Coming Forth by Night* also identified a new name for both Church and deity:

'Reconsecrate my Temple and my Order in the true name of Set. No longer will I accept the bastard title of a Hebrew fiend.'

There were also other instructions for the new magical epoch:

'When I came first to this world, I gave to you my great pentagram, timeless measure of beauty through proportion. And it was shown inverse, that creation and change be exalted above rest and preservation.

'With the years my pentagram was corrupted, yet time has not the power to destroy it. Its position was restored by the Church of Satan, but its essence was dimmed with a Moorish name, and the perverse letters of the Hebrews, and the goat of decadent Khar. During the Age of Satan I allowed this curious corruption, for it was meant to do me honour as I was then perceived.

'But this is now my Aeon, and my pentagram is again to be pure in its splendour. Cast aside the corruptions, that the pentagram of Set may shine forth. Let all who seek me be never without it, openly and with pride, for by it shall I know them.

'Let the one who aspires to my knowledge be called by the name Setian.'[3]

Aquino says that this revelation led the priesthood of the former Church of Satan into completely new areas of enquiry:

'The founders of the Temple of Set knew very little about Egyptology and we had to go and find out who Set was, and why something like this should be happening. We found out some very interesting things. The usual understanding of Set is that he was an evil god in the old Egyptian system — the benevolent father-god being Osiris and his evil antagonist, Set, who murdered him.

'In our research we discovered that this was in fact a much later corruption, and that the initial identity of Set had been that of the god of night, of the darkness, as opposed to the god of day, the sun. Set symbolized the *isolated psyche*, the spark of life within the self, a creative force in the universe rather than an enemy figure, an inspiration for the individual consciousness...'

So, how have things changed since the dramatic days of 1975?

Lilith Sinclair, Aquino's partner in the Temple of Set, says simply that the new Order is 'the Church of Satan grown up'. Rituals under Anton La Vey's jurisdiction, she says, were presented 'on a very self-indulgent, materialistic level' and Satan himself was 'more a symbol than an actual reality'.

Now, says Lilith, the contact with the Prince of Darkness is tangible and powerful — 'a very quiet, serene, beautiful touching of minds'. She emphasizes that there is no pact signed in blood but instead a type of private vow:

'It's done on an individual basis, and it's something that I myself wanted to do.'

The individual relationship of Order members with Set is in fact the core focus of the Temple, to such an extent that there are no prescribed rituals or dogmas, no central Temple, and no specific vows. Each Setian has his or her own private quest and must work alone. And whereas most forms of devotional mysticism and religion advocate the surrender of the ego to the godhead, awareness of self is maintained at all times. When communicating with Set, says Lilith, 'You retain your individuality... but at the same time you are linked with the essence of the Prince of Darkness. It's a natural exchange and flow of energy, of mind awareness.'

The Temple of Set is, indeed, quite cerebral, undoubtedly reflecting the intellectual background of Michael Aquino and his emphasis on rational thought.

Aquino divides the manifested universe broadly into three levels of reality. In the everyday world — the so-called 'natural order' — we obscure cause and effect relationships, and the scientific method and technology are based on this. At another level further removed, and exemplified by Plato — whom Aquino much admires — is philosophic thought. This is characterized by deduction and induction: the power of reason buttressed by observable fact. And beyond this, at an even more profound level, is the world of magical reality. There is a spiritual and psychic dimension to the human constitution, says Aquino, and this transcends the more mundane levels of existence. However, where he differs from Christians, mystics and pagans — whom for this purpose he lumps together — is in his belief that the psychic dimension *separates* mankind from the rest of Nature. Mystics and occultists alike are content to subsume their individual self-hood in a wash of cosmic consciousness — a type of surrender to a higher force. Christians, he feels, are bogged down with feelings of guilt and hypocrisy, endorsing 'hackneyed moral standards' in an effort to appease God.

For Aquino, Satanism is unique because it advocates 'personal behaviour that is essentially self-determined'. And while at this stage the Temple of Set has fewer than a hundred members worldwide, Aquino is convinced that his path is essentially correct. 'Other religions,' says the Temple's introductory screed, are 'erroneous in principle and therefore unworthy of peer status.' If this seems arrogant, Aquino has his reasons:

'All conventional religions, including the pagan ones, are simply a variation on the theme of reunion and submergence of the self within the natural universe. So from our point of view it really makes no difference whether you pray to a father god or to a mother goddess — or to an entire gaggle of gods and goddesses! You're still wishing for their acceptance. You're waiting for them to put their arms around you and say,

"You belong. You are part of us. You can relax. We will take care of you. We approve of you. We endorse you..." The Satanist or black magician does not seek that kind of submergence of the self. We do not seek to have our decisions and our morality approved or validated by any higher god or being. We take responsibility unto ourselves.'

This, of course, begs the question of how the Satanist stands in relation to Set, who is presumably a being on a higher plane.

'We do not pray to the Devil or Satan or Set,' says Aquino in distinguishing his path from other religious and occult philosophies, 'we have no desires or wishes that we expect to be granted by some sort of divinity. We consider Set to be our activating force and the entire notion of good and evil is something which is determined by human beings themselves. We cannot pass the responsibility to *any* god, whether it is a so-called benevolent god or a so-called evil god.'

Those who have explored the many different branches of self-development in the Human Potential movement will recognize here the self-actualizing philosophy served up in a different form. As Werner Erhard, founder of EST, has said in his workshops and lectures, we should all learn to take responsibility for our own being, create our own reality. Others have urged us to 'own our own lives' and become independent psychic powers in a universe essentially of our own making. All of which implies, of course, that man himself is god. Lilith Sinclair puts it somewhat more arrogantly:

'We regard ourselves very highly because we feel we are superior beings. We feel that we are gaining the knowledge of a deeper universe.'

Michael Aquino endorses this also. The Temple of Set, he says simply, has introduced a new philosophical epoch, 'a state of mental evolution'.

When one talks with Michael Aquino and Lilith Sinclair, however, there still remains an unexplained factor, a missing component. Their quest for self-hood and individual growth is undoubtedly a mature spiritual approach which takes man beyond mental crutches and the restrictions of dogma directly into the dark infinity of space — a variant perhaps on the Void, or *Sunyata*, of the Mahayana Buddhists. But why do they surround themselves with images of medieval demons, gargoyles and grimacing goblins? Why perpetuate the now clichéd Satanic symbolism of wearing red and black? And why the tufted eyebrows and the nurtured widow's peak — a clear identification with the medieval Devil? Why too the inscribed Nazi dagger?

In his defence, Michael Aquino says that 'everything comes back to the power of the self, and all of our ritual implements, all of our ritual chamber accessories, are reflections of the power of the individual self.'

This in turn leads us to another dimension of the Temple of Set which is possibly very revealing indeed — its connection with the S.S. and Nazi Germany.

The specific links between the Setian philosophy and the magical practices of the esoteric Nazi group led by Heinrich Himmler are difficult to trace but are present, nevertheless. Although Michael Aquino states very clearly that there are many aspects of the former Nazi regime which are repugnant to him, there is also a powerful attraction — the feeling that the Nazis were able to summon an extraordinary psychic force which was misdirected — but need not have been. Over and beyond this there is also the recurrent Satanic commitment to the idea that man — *super* man, or *initiated* man — is God, and that as such may discover a way of living forever, becoming a bright star in the firmament.

In his Temple newsletter, *Runes*[4], Aquino makes the comment that 'the successful magician must develop and ultimately master the ability to make himself the *constant*, and everything else *variable*, subject to his Will' (my italics). This means the magician 'moves gradually towards an existence in which time becomes your servant and not your master' and it also, says Aquino, 'will enable you to conquer death'.

He quotes from the well known classic of Egyptian thought, *Her-Bak*, which includes a sage's answer to the young priest Her-Bak's inquiry about life and death:

'What is life? It is a form of the divine presence. It is the power, immanent in created things, to change themselves by successive destructions of form until the spirit or activating force of the original life-stream is freed. This power resides in the very nature of things...It is the spiritual aim of all human life to attain a state of consciousness that is independent of bodily circumstance.'

Aquino makes the point that the Nazis tried to transfer the life-consciousness from the individual to the state, but the members of Himmler's esoteric group understood the process on a deeper level:

'Most Nazis were able to achieve (the transfer of consciousness) only in a mundane sense — in a kind of ecstatic selflessness created and sustained by propaganda. But the "monk-knights" of the pre-war S.S. could disdain, even willingly embrace, the death of the individual human body because the consciousness had been transferred to a larger life-form — that of the Hegelian state — and individual sacrifice towards the strengthening of that life-form would actually contribute towards one's immortality... All of the individual-death references in the S.S., such as the *Totenkopf* insignia and ritual pledges of "Faithfulness unto death", were in fact, arrogant affirmations of immortality.'[5]

This leads us to a magical ceremony undertaken by Michael Aquino in a chamber in Wewelsburg Castle, beneath the Marble Hall used by Himmler's magical order — the Ahnenerbe. Wewelsburg Castle is located in German Westphalia, on the site of ancient Saxon fortifications. The castle in its present form was constructed by Archbishop Theodore von Fuerstenberg in 1604-7 but was damaged by Swedish artillery during the Thirty Years War. In 1815, the North Tower was struck and nearly destroyed by lightning, and the castle fell into neglect. However in 1933 the S.S. acquired Wewelsburg as its inner sanctum and Himmler began a programme of reconstruction. One of his innovations was to build a circular chamber known as the Marmorsaal (Marble Hall) to replace the original chapel of the castle. According to Aquino, it was inspired by the Hall of the Grail created by Alfred Roller, on Hitler's instructions, for the 1934 production of *Parsifal* at Bayreuth.

Set in the red Italian marble floor, is a dark green marble disc from which extend twelve rune-motifs. The design as a whole, while usually categorized as a 'solar symbol', is actually a secret magical sigil from an esoteric order, the Westphaelischen Femgerichte, known usually as the Vehm. As such, the room was the ideal meeting place for the Ahnenerbe who believed they were part of the same magical tradition.

Michael Aquino clearly perceives the inner group of priests and priestesses of the Temple of Set to be the magical successors, in turn, to the Ahnenerbe and Vehm, and it was beneath the Marble Hall, in a secret chamber known as the Hall of the Dead, that he chose to perform another ritual invocation to the Prince of Darkness in 1982.

We do not have the details of Aquino's invocation for, as with his earlier revelation from Set, there are aspects which remain strictly private. What we do know, however, is that during the ceremony Aquino confirmed his belief that magically *man stands apart from the universe.* In his own words: 'The Wewelsburg working asserts that Life is conceptually contrary to Nature... and "unnatural" in its very essence.'[6]

For Aquino, then, the essential task of the magical initiate is to evolve to god-like proportions, subjecting the 'natural' universe to his will. Man owes his special status on earth to 'the deliberate intervention of a non-natural intelligence (known to us as Set) and the respect accorded to the Prince of Darkness is simply an acknowledgement that he inspires man to strive ever higher in his quest for dominance.'

Included in this pursuit, as mentioned earlier, is the attempt to conquer death. Whereas mystics believe they must surrender their individuality to the godhead — *Nirvana, Sunyata, Ain Soph Aur* — Aquino maintains that this is ill-advised:

'We would simply say that what they have is a sort of sublimated death wish of the self and that we, unlike them, do not want to die.'

The key to Michael Aquino's philosophy of cheating death is also contained in the *Runes* newsletter. More intriguing even than the intricacies of genetic engineering, this involves manipulating the actual animating force in living things. Aquino believes that the psyche is neither dependent on, nor imprisoned by, the body, and that the mind of the magician is capable of reaching out 'towards the limitlessness of its conscious existence', a process which he calls *xeper*, an Egyptian word meaning 'to become'. Aquino expanded this idea from a statement contained in Anton La Vey's *Satanic Bible* (The Book of Lucifer):

'If a person has been vital throughout his life and has fought to the end for his earthly existence, it is this ego which will refuse to die, even after the expiration of the flesh which housed it. It is this vitality that will allow the Satanist to peel through the curtain of darkness and death, and remain earthbound.'

The broader implication, of course, is that the Satanist can meddle with life-forces governing the principles of birth, death and creation — manipulating the processes of Nature for his own ends.

Meanwhile, the final piece in the extraordinary jigsaw is provided by a bizarre and rather unwholesome experiment in necromancy undertaken by Aquino and La Vey. This took place in August 1973, when the two occultists were still working together, and represented an attempt to bring a dead person back to life. In this case the corpse was none other than that of ill-fated movie-star Marilyn Monroe, and the aim of the sorcery was to summon her *anima* to take form once again from the natural elements into which her life-force had dissipated. Both Aquino and La Vey were interested in a 'psychic evaluation' of the events leading to the actress's death since there had been rumours of foul play by the CIA following Monroe's alleged love affair with President Kennedy. Aquino describes the extraordinary episode in his privately published book, *The Church of Satan*:

'Anton asked that we both direct our thoughts to the bedroom of the house in the Brentwood cul-de-sac...it was in this bedroom that Marilyn's corpse had been discovered. For perhaps 15 minutes there was no change in the still atmosphere. Then I noticed that the chamber, already cold, seemed even more chill. Gazing slowly about the room, I saw that a change of a more material type had also taken place:

the top of the low bed was now distorted with uneven indentations along its right side... Within the impressions on the bed there gradually appeared the nude body of a woman, face-down, contorted, and irregularly streaked or blotched with what seemed to be blood... The materialization of this body was accompanied by a mental sensation of "queasiness" — as though one had encountered something corrupt or unclean...

'Anton La Vey may have known the details of Marilyn Monroe's death, but I myself did not. The following year, when Robert Slatzer's book *The Life and Curious Death of Marilyn Monroe* was published, I learned that the actress's body had been discovered nude and face-down on her bed. Suspicion had been aroused by how *uncontorted* the body was — not characteristic of death by barbiturate poisoning — and of course there was no visible blood. It was the contorted and bloodied state of the *anima* that told Anton what he wanted to know.'[7]

The Temple of Set is a most unusual organization and not a little bizarre. For example, ten years after the necromantic experiment described above, Michael Aquino and Lilith Sinclair replicated the magical working outside the actress's home in Brentwood and they intend to follow it up with a further working some time in the future. Their interim findings have not been released to their fellow members of the Temple of Set.

To even begin to understand Michael Aquino and his Setian colleagues one has to amalgamate sources as varied and far-ranging as classical Greek philosophy, ancient Egyptian mythology, medieval and modern Satanism and, as we have seen, the magical practices of a Nazi secret society. Aquino himself is complex, intellectual and self-assured — convinced, in fact, that his particular type of magical exploration goes beyond the scope of orthodox mysticism and religion. In this respect, he may well be right.

Just how history will judge Michael Aquino and the Temple of Set is difficult to tell, and from his point of view it matters little anyway. As he has written in his newsletter, the Temple of Set has no apparent peers and modern Satanism is bound to appear elusive and mysterious to lesser mortals unable to understand it. Lilith explains this perspective:

'Satanism and the Temple of Set appeal to people so powerfully because they take you out of the little box that most people are imprisoned in and put you into a universe where your opportunities and your visioning, your perception, are limitless. You find yourself in a completely different world with endless corridors of time to explore and you only limit yourself by what you think you can and cannot do. It's a very powerful thing. It's total freedom...'

1. Michael Aquino, *The Crystal Tablet of Set*, 1983, p.23.

2. Aquino p.23.

3. Aquino p.27.

4. *Runes* Vol. II: 6, 1984.

5. *Runes* id.

6. *Runes* Vol. I: 2, 1983.

7. Michael Aquino, *The Church of Satan*, 1983, p.193.

CHAPTER 5
New Frontiers

Although occult beliefs and practices vary enormously —
from the earthy pantheism of Wicca through to the self-
oriented, power-based creed of the Temple of Set — most
philosophies of this type have a fundamental, underlying
purpose: the achievement of new and heightened awareness.
This may vary simply from a general attunement to Nature,
through to the expression of one's own divinity — the idea
that man and woman can become as gods.

Reasons for the appeal of occult philosophy are not hard
to find and, indeed, the ongoing popularity of magical beliefs
is one of the many possible responses to the dominance of
science in the modern era. One could argue, in fact, that the
development of technology has actually heightened the
increasing interest in the occult.

The overriding belief system which most educated people
incline towards in the modern world, at least in theory, is a
credo of precision and measurement. Science and technology
have, without doubt, banished God from the machine. The
concepts which modern western man is now urged to hold
most dearly — from an increasingly automated lifestyle to

President Reagan's 'Star Wars' programme — are those which are seemingly justified by scientific research, by a coherent rationale, by seeking a logical solution to a problem. This is very much a reductionist approach to life, and any mystery that might have been brought to the human equation has now, for the most part, been reduced to a discussion of DNA molecules, genetic variables and the synapses of the brain. Our lives and individuality are simply a biochemical by-product of a broader, more general formula, and — for the mechanistic psychologists of the B. F. Skinner persuasion — man is little more than a sophisticated robot whose behaviour can be measured, tested, evaluated and programmed. According to this perspective, we live in a world of stimulus and response exemplified, on a simpler level, by rats in mazes.

Such a viewpoint is alien to the world of mystics, occultists and neopagans, for whom the phenomenal world is only the most obvious manifestation of a much broader — and to a larger extent, imperceptible — universe. The physical world — within Kabbalistic, magical and mystical belief alike — is considered the least real because it is the furthest removed from the sacred energy source which sustains the universe, the most illusory because it is simply an outer shell of a profound and indescribable mystery.

It is interesting to note though, that the hard veneer of scientific certainty is beginning to crack, partly because advances in quantum physics have confirmed that matter is really space and energy and that physical boundaries are less distinct than we previously thought. Furthermore, quantum theory has demonstrated the role of the participant observer in evaluating physical reality, thereby highlighting the variable and subjective nature of human perception.

Now, for the first time since the pioneering work of

William James and Carl Jung, psychology is beginning to turn away from behaviour to *consciousness* as the key focus for understanding man. For if we can understand the nature of human consciousness we begin to understand the sources of human creativity, intuition and belief, and we gain new insights into the nature of values and aesthetic ideals. We get closer, in fact, to understanding important aspects of humanity which we have always known were real but were unable to measure.

The change of heart we are describing here can be attributed substantially to the rise, since the late 1960s, of a new school of social science. Known as transpersonal psychology, it has adopted broader boundaries of inquiry than earlier reductionist disciplines and is casting further afield to establish its perspectives.

Often referred to now as the 'fourth force' in psychology — succeeding and complementing classical psychoanalytic thought, behavioural psychology and humanistic psychology which came before it — the transpersonal school regards man as a total being, a synthesis of body, mind and spirit. In so doing, it has found itself encroaching into areas of human belief and expression which, until recently, had been dismissed by the scientific community as religious, mystical and irrational. According to the transpersonal viewpoint these aspects of human expression are a valid part of man's being and represent a dimension of his existence that needs to be acknowledged.

This does not mean that somehow science is becoming 'soft'. A recent conference of the International Transpersonal Association in Bombay attracted among its lecturers such distinguished scientists as biochemist Rupert Sheldrake, Yale neurosurgeon Karl Pribram and physicist Fritjof Capra. It is more a recognition that western philosophy needs a larger frame of reference — a blending, perhaps, of science and mysticism. As psychologist Frances Vaughan said at Bombay, 'The transpersonal perspective has been emerging from the needed integration of ancient wisdom and modern science. Science without wisdom can destroy the world; wisdom without science remains ineffectual.'[1]

Dr Vaughan also made the point that the transpersonal approach is a 'meta-perspective, an attempt to learn from all different perspectives. It does not attempt to impose a new belief system or a new metaphysics, but rather to see the relationship between existing world views in order to create something that can be truly transformational in our world.'

It is clear from Dr Vaughan's comments that transpersonal psychology has much in common with the esoteric traditions but it did not derive from them historically. This school of thought, in fact, has its source in humanistic psychology and the work of two pioneering social scientists: Abraham Maslow and Anthony Sutich. Unfortunately, neither lived to see the consequences of their vision, Maslow dying in 1970 and Sutich in 1976.

Maslow was for many years Professor of Psychology at Brandeis University and had originally trained in psychoanalytic theory and gestalt psychology. However he noticed that many of his academic colleagues seemed preoccupied with disease and mental disorders and felt his research should, instead, focus on individuals who were healthy and creative. From this orientation Maslow derived the idea of self-actualization which he referred to as 'the full use and exploitation of talents, capacities, and potentialities'. He also noticed that often individuals who seemed capable of self-actualizing were also people with a spontaneous, creative flair and capable of mystical or 'peak' experiences.

In 1954 Maslow began to develop a mailing list to maintain links with psychologists who were sympathetic to his approach. At that time in the United States most social scientists were trenchantly behaviouristic and by 1957 Maslow's list still comprised fewer than 125 people.

However, good things did come from it, for it was primarily through Maslow's contact with Californian psychologist and counsellor, Anthony Sutich, that the American Association of Humanistic Psychology was established.

Sutich was a self-trained psychologist and worked assisting nurses at the Palo Alto Society for the Blind. Despite crippling rheumatoid arthritis, Sutich maintained a private practice in Palo Alto and encouraged his clients to think in terms of psychological 'growth'. He was particularly interested in group therapy 'with emphasis on spiritual as well as emotional development'.

Since the 1940s he had studied Eastern religion, and he met Swami Ashokananda through friends who were members of the Vedanta Society of San Francisco. He was also familiar with the works of Ramakrishna, Akhilananda and Vivekananda, and in 1948 attended a series of lectures given by Krishnamurti. Sutich later met Alan Watts in the San Francisco Bay Area and instructed him in counselling techniques. As a result, Watts began to combine mysticism, Zen Buddhism and psychotherapy in a form of 'non-directive counselling' which allowed patients to work on paradoxes and contradictions in their everyday lives. At the same time, Sutich was stimulated by Watts to read more widely in the mystical literature.

Sutich met Maslow briefly in 1949, and a few years later, in 1957, Maslow wrote to him encouraging him to found a new journal with special emphasis on such human attributes as 'creativeness, love, self-actualization, "higher values", ego-transcendence, objectivity, autonomy, responsibility and psychological health'.

Maslow was now referring to his approach as the 'third force' in psychology and was attracting support from such distinguished psychologists as Rollo May, Carl Rogers, Gardner Murphy, Erich Fromm, among others. The first issue of *The Journal of Humanistic Psychology* appeared in April 1961 and coincided with the establishment of the American Association of Humanistic Psychology.

The Association grew steadily and both Sutich and Maslow began to widen their range of contacts. In April 1958 Sutich had written to a researcher named Dr A. M. Hubbard for information on LSD, and later told Maslow of the apparent links between LSD and peak experiences. Sutich subsequently met Dr Timothy Leary but was surprised to find that Leary was using psychedelics outside the therapeutic context.

Then, in January 1966, Sutich went to a humanistic theology seminar in Big Sur, California. Among those attending were a number of Jesuit theologians who were asked by a lecturer whether they had ever had a mystical experience, and whether it was Church policy to encourage that sort of thing. To both questions the theologians replied 'no' and Sutich noted in his diary that he was 'very surprised' by these answers.

Shortly afterwards Sutich attended two further meetings in Big Sur, designed to highlight the shortcomings of humanistic psychology. Sutich came to the conclusion that 'the concept of self-actualization was no longer comprehensive enough' for, as a therapist, he 'could hardly avoid the question of his own orientation in relation to ultimate goals, mystical experiences, peak experiences...' He felt that Esalen Institute and other 'personal growth' centres then emerging in the United States might become 'the American equivalent of Zen monasteries' and he was now convinced that he should blend mysticism and psychology both in his personal frameworks and in his professional practice.

Meanwhile in September 1967, Maslow gave an address to the San Francisco Unitarian Church in which, for the first time, he made reference to the 'fourth force' in psychology — a major development from humanistic psychology. Maslow had recently completed an article in which he argued that 'the value life (spiritual, religious, philosophical) is an aspect of human biology. The spiritual life is then part of the human essence. It is a defining characteristic of human nature, without which human nature is not full human nature. It is part of the Real Self, of one's identity, of one's inner core, or one's specieshood, of full humanness.'[2] Three months later Maslow expressed the view that the word 'transpersonal', meaning 'beyond the personal', was an ideal one to describe the new psychology and in a letter to Sutich he wrote:

'... this word says what we are all trying to say, that is, beyond individuality, beyond the development of the individual person into something which is more inclusive than the individual person, or which is bigger than he is.'

Here Maslow had in mind a psychology which could embrace the spiritual and mystical dimensions of man and, in particular, 'peak experiences' which swept a person into transcendental states beyond the ego-based personality.

Not surprisingly, Esalen Institute in Big Sur was to play a major role in the development of the transpersonal perspective. For here, thought Maslow, was a centre dedicated to exploring the furthest reaches of human consciousness. Here was a spiritual but non-denominational environment broad enough in its vision to charter the parameters of human potential. And it also happened to be located in beautiful and awesome surroundings that could hardly help but touch the spirit.

As you drive north from San Simeon, the Californian coastline becomes increasingly craggy and precipitous. Highway 1 soon transforms into a narrow, winding course-way with spectacular cliff-edges falling away to the left and the sudden and dramatic Santa Lucia mountains rising up on the right. Wildflowers and lichen provide dashes of colour here and there, but much of the terrain is rugged and severe. However there are pockets of beautiful greenery as well — regal cypresses which grow in precarious positions, on impossible ledges, above sharp rock spurs which jut out from the crashing sea below.

Big Sur is only superficially tamed by man. Highway 1 was only completed in 1937 and even now is often blocked by falls of stone or by pockets of fog which roll in from the ocean. It is also a route which dictates its own pace, for drivers who venture here do not speed along but wind carefully and humbly round the seemingly endless successions of hairpin bends, ever aware of the precarious balance between man, cliff-edge and ocean.

The Spanish called this region after the river El Rio Grande de Sur, and the jagged, weaving coastline extends for some 80 kilometres — almost as far north as Carmel and Monterey. The town of Big Sur itself is still only a small settlement, famous mostly for its Nepenthe Inn — a vegetarian restaurant with impressive wooden sculptures and a wonderful view to the south. The controversial novelist, Henry Miller, also spent many years living near here as a recluse.

Esalen Institute is located between Big Sur township and the charming hamlet of Lucia. One comes upon it suddenly, and it too rests literally on the cliff edge. A place of considerable natural beauty, it is now part of local folklore. It is also, as many have said, the birthplace of the 'new paradigm'.

Esalen Institute used to be known simply as Slate's Hot Springs. The land was acquired in 1910 by Henry Murphy, a doctor from Salinas, and he built the dwelling now known as the Big House as a holiday home. By the late 1950s, however, the land had fallen into disrepair and Slate's Hot Springs was being visited mostly by Henry Miller and his circle of bohemian friends. Old Dr Murphy had long since died, the Big House was being maintained by a young macho writer named Hunter Thompson, and nothing much was happening except occasional brawls among the locals.

In 1962, however, things changed when Dr Murphy's son Michael and a Zen Buddhism enthusiast named Richard Price drove down to the property to have a new look at it. They came up with an idea that was to have far-reaching consequences — Big Sur Hot Springs, as it was now called, could be a meeting place for different spiritual traditions and for the exploration of consciousness. Philosophers, writers and mystics could come here to impart their knowledge and share their experiences. It could become a very special place indeed.

With this vision, the spirit of Esalen was born, although the Springs would still be known by their old name for three more years. The Lodge, a meeting room on the property up the hill from the Big House, became the centre for seminars, and early visitors included Alan Watts, Aldous Huxley, Paul Tillich and, as we have already mentioned, Abraham Maslow. By the mid-1960s Esalen had become associated with an even broader range of famous visitors, including encounter therapist Will

Schutz, Indian musician Ali Akbar Khan, environmentalist Buckminster Fuller, bodywork pioneer Ida Rolf, and the distinguished founder of gestalt therapy, Fritz Perls, who actually took up residence. Esalen soon acquired a reputation as an idyllic therapeutic hideaway; a place to enjoy weekend seminars and experiential workshops, and discover your inner being. It was a place to get in touch with your feelings, 'awaken your senses', reach out to your partner, and enjoy the communal hot-tub experience on the cliff edge above the Pacific Ocean.

Not that everyone at Esalen was mystical, however. Fritz Perls, in particular, despised this aspect of the personal growth movement and endeavoured to bring his own, much more confronting, and sometimes brutal, style of therapy to the fore. There were also personal rivalries between seminar leaders, competitive ploys to attract workshop participants and a certain amount of unfortunate politicking with the media. Despite these problems, however, Esalen was emerging as the focus of the so-called 'new consciousness' in America, and was to become home to almost every new therapy under the sun.

These days the range of experiential workshops offered at Esalen is enormous. People come to learn techniques of Tai Chi, massage, Zen, hypnosis, dance, shamanism, Taoism, 'creative sexuality' and Feldenkrais bodywork, or to attend lectures on gnosticism, Findhorn or feminist religions. The range is diverse and ever-changing, and a handsome catalogue, issued periodically, announces the forthcoming events for the year.

Esalen is now somewhat less controversial than it used to be. Perhaps the general public has a greater familiarity with mysticism, the various martial arts therapies, and the notion of 'health for the whole person', but whether this is true or not Esalen, in particular, is no longer perceived as a place for hippies and members of the counter-culture. If anything, it has become rather tame and quite decidedly middleclass.

In recent years it has been customary at Esalen to appoint a scholar-in-residence, an academic in tune with the general philosophy of the Human Potential movement and able to contribute to new areas of consciousness research. The present incumbent is a Czechoslovakian psychiatrist, and close friend of the late Anthony Sutich, Dr Stanislav Grof.

Grof is a man of considerable distinction, a scientist who has specialized in researching altered states of consciousness for most of his professional career. He is also a former president of the International Transpersonal Association.

Born in Prague in 1931, Grof studied medicine and in due course received his PhD from the Czechoslovakian Academy of Science. He then began research into the psychotherapeutic uses of LSD — a controversial line of enquiry which he continued after migrating to the United States in 1967. Dr Grof worked in Baltimore at the Maryland Psychiatric Research Center and then became an assistant professor at Johns Hopkins University. One of his particular fields of interest was research into the use of psychedelics for easing the pain of terminal cancer patients.

Unfortunately, by the mid-1970s, LSD had become too controversial politically, and scientific research into its medical applications was all but abandoned. Dr Grof felt this to be extremely unfortunate since he was finding the LSD work a legitimate way of probing the unconscious mind as well as throwing light on cultural patterns in general. As he wrote in 1979:

'The theoretical importance of the data from psychedelic research extends far beyond the realms of psychiatry and psychology. It is also of immediate or potential relevance for a broad spectrum of other disciplines, including anthropology, sociology, politics, general medicine, obstetrics, thanatology, religion, philosophy, mythology and art.'

It was also clear, said Dr Grof, that the LSD data 'could contribute significantly to our understanding of the nature of reality.'[3]

At first Grof's views seemed paradoxical to his colleagues. After all, wasn't LSD an artificial substance, a potent psychedelic whose main effect was to stimulate hallucinations — often on a large scale? And wasn't a psychedelic simply a trigger for illusory states of mind, a way to induce a 'model psychosis'?

Dr Grof had found this to be a simplistic view, although when LSD research was at its height most psychiatrists were evaluating it for the light it might shed on mental disorders, especially schizophrenia. There was also the debate — spurred on by Timothy Leary, Richard Alpert and Alan Watts — over whether LSD was really a type of sacrament, offering a path to instant enlightenment through 'chemical mysticism'. Leary, in particular, was urging his enthusiastic followers in the counter-culture to 'turn on, tune in and drop out'.

Grof's broad finding was that LSD simply triggered the mind to manifest, that LSD didn't actually *produce* anything of itself. Expressing this point more scientifically Grof wrote in his major work *Realms of the Human Unconscious*:

'I have not been able to discover during the analyses of my data any distinct pharmacological effects of LSD in humans that would be constant and invariant and could therefore be considered drug-specific. At the present time, I consider LSD to be a powerful unspecific amplifier or catalyst of biochemical and physiological processes in the brain.'[4]

In other words, LSD was a valuable way of probing the patterns of consciousness and of producing a 'cartography of the mind'. LSD could only release what was in there already.

Grof now found that the LSD research had led him to deeper levels of consciousness than he expected:

'I was brought up and educated as a Freudian analyst and so when we started doing the LSD work I expected that we'd be mostly working with biographical material. I was looking for a tool that would somehow bring out the unconscious material much faster, so that it would deepen and intensify psychoanalysis. To my surprise people would not stay in the biographical domain which, according to western psychology, is considered to be the only domain available — memories from childhood and the individual unconscious. Without any programming, and actually against my will, my subjects started moving into realms that hadn't been charted in psychoanalysis at all. The first encounter was powerful...death and birth. People started having sequences of dying and feeling reborn, frequently with details from their biological birth. But this experience of death then reversed and became like a gateway into the transcendental, the archetypal — the transpersonal as we call it now. All this material emerged as a great surprise for me.'

Grof now came to the view that there were basically four levels in the psychedelic encounter with the mind. The first of these, experienced at the most superficial level, involved sensory phenomena — an intensification of colours and geometrical patterns, and often increased awareness of sounds, humming, chimes and so on. The next level was what Grof calls 'biographical', and its content included unresolved conflicts from one's present life, childhood problems and occasionally traumatic memories from an earlier phase, diphtheria, whooping cough, cases of near drowning, major operations or injuries. 'These,' says Grof, 'are the unfinished gestalts or unresolved conflicts' — which need to be brought to the surface and worked through. Proceeding still deeper, one now came to the third level — that of perinatal experiences. These relate to the birth experience and as Grof writes in *Realms of the Human Unconscious,* 'are a manifestation of a deep level of the unconscious that is clearly beyond the reach of classical Freudian techniques.'[5] Grof found that LSD could trigger memories of birth that clearly were not illusory. Subjects were sometimes able to verify details of their birth experiences which emerged during sessions — information which was not available to them in their conscious state but which was released at a deep level of inner probing.

The fourth level of mind accessed through LSD was the most important of all, 'the very vast domain which we call the "transpersonal"'. Grof had been instrumental, with Maslow, in coining this word, and explained further what was meant by it:

'"Transpersonal" means transcending the personal — that which is beyond the usual body/ego framework. It also refers to experiences going back to the womb, ancestral memories, Jungian archetypes, mythological sequences and past-life recall — experiences which transcend spatial boundaries rather than temporal boundaries.'

It is in this area that Grof finds a link between mystical states and the principles of quantum physics — both of which emphasize the interconnectedness of all forms in the manifested universe. The sense of separation, of distinctiveness, says Grof, simply falls away at this level of awareness:

'Here the mandatory boundaries of the body seem to be melting and the person has the experience, perhaps, of fusing with other people, or becoming other people, becoming animals, becoming plant life and, in some cases, having telepathic experiences. Sometimes too there are mythological or archetypal sequences, portraying something that this culture would not normally regard as part of objective reality or the phenomenal world.'

After 20 years of LSD research Dr Grof believes he has uncovered valuable patterns for consciousness research, and his unique work has not gone unnoticed. Pulitzer Prize-winning scientist Carl Sagan notes in *The Dragons of Eden* that, 'Grof probably has more scientific experience in the effects of psychedelic drugs on patients than anyone else', and distinguished parapsychologist Dr Stanley Krippner has referred to Grof as the 'world's foremost psychedelic researcher'. This recognition, however, could do little to make the LSD controversy disappear in the mid-1970s when the issue of psychedelic therapy was coming to a climax. While Grof clearly felt that he was discovering tangible data about the human mind, and not simply documenting illusory states, it was evident that new methods of tapping transpersonal states of consciousness would have to be developed. The result was a special technique involving hyperventilation breathing and music — a therapy which Grof now practises in his workshops at Esalen.

Superficially, Grof Breathing, as it is now known, resembles a more widely known technique called Rebirthing — a therapy evolved by Leonard Orr in California during the early 1970s. Both derive substantially from *pranayama* — the Indian yoga of breath — which employs a connected breathing rhythm to produce an altered state of consciousness. In both

therapies the subject lies horizontally in a comfortable position with a facilitator, or helper, sitting nearby to assist in any
crisis. The session begins as the subject engages in rhythmic
in-and-out breathing, with no pauses in between. As Orr has
written, 'You merge with your breath, flowing, glowing,
soaring, relaxing profoundly, your mind melting into your
spirit, surging, awakening your inner being and the quiet
sounds of your soul...'

In Grof Breathing, however, the technique is somewhat
more intense and the results more sudden and dramatic. The
breathing is accompanied by recorded music which is chosen
to reflect different phases of the cathartic process. As Grof
explains: 'The music is the vehicle itself, so at the beginning
we start with some very activating, powerful music. Then,
maybe an hour into the session, we move into a kind of
culminating, "breakthrough" type of music — for example
using the sound of bells or similar, very powerful, transcendental sounds.' His musical selections are indeed varied —
African tribal rhythms, Sufi chants, Indian ragas, Japanese
flute or the relaxing piano of Steven Halpern. However, the
breathing itself is also vitally important.

Paradoxically, hyperventilation breathing actually reduces
the amount of oxygen transmitted to the cortex of the brain,
producing a natural 'high'. The technique simulates the experience of mystics who live in high altitudes where the air is
more rarified. As Grof says casually, the workshops are ideal
for those who can't make a trip to the Himalayas...

The workshop is held on this occasion in a large wooden hut
close to the cliff-edge, above the hot tubs. Around 20 people,
most of them in their twenties or early thirties, have come to
participate, and some are here for the first time. They are

from many different countries — Carlos, short and dark, somewhat nervous, from Spain; Heidi, golden-haired and almost ethereal, from Austria; Helmut, energetic and boyish, from Germany. Also attending are Andrea, a psychology student from Australia and Helen, a platinum-blonde legal secretary from Dallas.

Grof explains the basic breathing procedure, divides the group into pairs — one member experiencing, the other assisting — and the music begins. The result is dramatic. Intense rhythms build up, layer upon layer, resonating through the room and soon there are groans, writhings, chokings, and physical contortions, lunging movements from side to side, sexual thrusting postures, thumpings of legs and elbows, and even symbolic returns to the foetus. There is an intense pouring forth of emotions — hidden fears, stifled anxieties, forgotten traumas — all of these feelings surging simultaneously to the surface. Grof, meanwhile, moves rapidly from one subject to another, helping each person in turn to move through 'blockages', or overcome traumatic images that have flooded into consciousness. For over an hour the process continues. At times Carlos seems to be wrestling with an inner demon as he writhes on the ground and then suddenly sits bolt upright, clawing at space. Helen twists and turns on her mat, 'exploring', as she later explains, 'different realities'. Heidi, meanwhile, experiences alternating moods of joyfulness and grief, and lies quietly sobbing as waves of emotions ripple through her body. For her, as she later tells it, the encounter had several dimensions: 'I felt very unhappy, I was crying and I basically wanted to be very close to my mother ... to be protected again by her. And then, after some time, I switched to another image, and that took me back — it was very ancient. I think it was back in the Stone Age. I saw myself lying down... ready to die, and there was a frightening odour — but there was actually a very warm and positive feeling around me because a lot of black people were dancing and it was such an expression of power...'

For her part, the session was finally positive: 'I feel much more connected with reality... usually we are fogged in our minds but there I could get a very clear picture.' Helen confirmed this also: 'At the end of my breathing I felt peaceful, euphoric, delighted I had done it.' Helmut described his inner journey as 'exciting... of having another perception of reality, taking more from life.' Carlos, on the other hand was troubled. He had had a complex and painful experience in which he was transformed into a sacrificial animal: 'I felt like a lion. I felt tired, I felt I had a kind of fever... and maybe that was the reason they were sacrificing me... they were going to kill me in a primitive way...'

Grof spent extended periods of time with Carlos as he would periodically come to an emotional climax, but Carlos in turn was finding it difficult to yield to the image of being killed. 'Face it,' Grof would urge him, 'Face it...' and eventually the conflict seemed to resolve itself. 'I felt that someone was taking my two hands and saying, "It doesn't matter how much you suffer, everything is going to be alright in the end",' says Carlos. 'Finally, I had the experience of being very positive, of feeling calm.'

For Grof, the trauma, the fear, the intense probing of inner states, are all eventually worthwhile. 'The birth experience,' he says, 'tends to open into what we call transpersonal experiences... it can be very beneficial, very transforming, very healing.' And the experience itself ends with a profound sense of peace. 'Many people tell us after a session like this that they have never been so relaxed in their whole life.'

Another frequent visitor to Esalen is Michael Harner, a professor of anthropology from New York, who conducts workshops on the way of the shaman. While for Grof, the path to altered states is through a combination of breathing and powerful recorded music, Harner's variant technique is to combine visualization methods with repetitive beating on a large flat drum.

Like Grof, Harner draws on ancient sources. Shamanism is a paleolithic form of trance religion which is even older than yoga. Like Grof, Harner has explored the use of psychedelics — he was once initiated by the Conibo Indians in the use of the 'visionary vine', Ayahuasca, and had a sacred encounter with mythical beings who claimed they were the true founders of the world. These days, however, Harner is interested in achieving similar states of consciousness without the use of psychedelics. No doubt this is partly a reflection of his position, for Harner is not only a visionary but also a respected academic — a former visiting professor at Columbia, Yale and Berkeley, and now resident at the New School for Social Research, New York.

He is a large, bear-like man with a fuzzy beard and dark, expressive eyes. He likes to grin, laugh and make jokes — resisting the guru or authority role thrust upon many key figures in the Human Potential movement. But even more impressively, he has drawn on many years of anthropological field-work, learning from the Indians rather than compartmentalizing their knowledge for purposes of research. He is now not only a distinguished anthropologist, but a shaman in his own right.

Harner was born in Washington D.C. but spent the early years of his childhood in South America. In 1956 he returned to do fieldwork among the Jivaro of the Ecuadorian Andes and between 1960 and 1961 visited the Conibo Indians of the Upper Amazon in Peru. His first period of fieldwork was conducted as 'an outside observer of the world of the shaman', he says, but his second endeavour — which included his psychedelic initiation among the Conibo — led him to pursue shamanism first-hand. In 1964 he returned to Ecuador to experience the supernatural world of the Jivaro in a more complete way.

After arriving at the former Spanish settlement of Macas, Harner made contact with his Jivaro guide, Akachu. Two days later he ventured with him northwards, crossing the Rio Upano and entering the forest. It was here that he told his Indian friend that he wished to acquire spirit-helpers, known to the Jivaro as *tsentsak*. Harner offered gifts to Akachu and was told that the first preparatory task was to bathe in the sacred waterfall. Later he was also presented with a magical pole, to ward off demons. Then, after an arduous journey to the waterfall, Harner was led into a dark recess behind the wall of spray — a cave known as 'the House of the Grandfathers' — and here he had to call out, attracting the attention of the ancestor spirits. He now had his first magical sensations: 'The wall of falling water became iridescent, a torrent of millions of liquid prisms. As they went by I had the continuous sensation of floating upward, as though they were stable and I was the one in motion.' It was, says Harner, 'like flying inside a mountain'.

Deeper in the jungle Akachu squeezed the juice of some psychedelic datura plants he had brought with him and asked Harner to drink it that night. Reassuring him, Akachu told him he was not to fear anything he might see, and if anything frightening did appear, he should run up and touch it!

That night was especially dramatic anyway — with pelting

rain, thunder and flashes of lightning — but after a while the effects of the datura became apparent and it was clear that something quite specific was going to happen.

Remembering his advice from Akachu, Harner charged at the visionary serpent with a stick. Suddenly the forest was empty and silent, and the monster had gone. Akachu later explained to Harner that this supernatural encounter was an important precursor to acquiring spirit-helpers. And his triumph over the serpent had confirmed that he was now an acceptable candidate for the path of the shaman.

Harner believes, as the Jivaro do, that the energizing force within any human being can be represented by what the Indians call a 'power animal'. One of the most important tasks of the shaman is to summon the power animal while in trance, and undertake visionary journeys with the animal as an ally. It is in such a way that one is able to explore the 'upper' and 'lower' worlds...

The shaman also learns techniques of healing which usually entail journeys to the spirit-world to obtain sources of 'magical energy'. These can then be transferred to sick or *dis*-spirited people in a ceremonial healing rite.[6]

After living with the Conibo and Jivaro, Michael Harner did further fieldwork among the Wintun and Pomo Indians in California, the Lakota Sioux of South Dakota, and the Coast Salish in Washington State. The techniques of applied shamanism which he now teaches in his workshops are a synthesis from many cultures, but they are true to the core essence of the tradition. 'Shamanism,' says Harner, 'takes us into the realms of myth and the Dreamtime... and in these experiences we are able to contact sources of power and use them in daily life.'

Tonight the shamanic workshop is being held at 'Kiva' — a large open room in an old tenement building in Canal Street, lower Manhattan. Most of the participants have experienced the shamanic journey before and are familiar with 'riding' the drumbeat into a state of meditative trance. They are wearing casual, comfortable clothing and have brought cushions and blankets, as well as hankerchiefs to drape over their eyes.

The session begins as Harner shakes his gourd rattle to the four quarters, summoning the 'spirits' to participate in the shamanic working. He also encourages the group to chant the Jivaro shaman-song:

> *I have spirits,*
> *Spirits have I . . .*
> *I have spirits,*
> *Spirits have I . . .*
> *I have spirits,*
> *Spirits have I . . .*
> *I, I, I,*

The participants, meanwhile, have formed themselves into the shape of a 'spirit-canoe', and each person present will visualize themselves riding in it, sailing down to the 'lower world'.

A *dis*-spirited woman named Regina lies in the centre of the canoe, and it is for her that the shamanizing will be done. After the initial procedures, Harner will join the canoe, lie beside her, and endeavour to journey on her behalf to the magical world. There he will obtain a healing spirit which can be transferred to her body, revitalizing her and making her well again.

Harner completes his circle of the spirit-canoe, lays down

his gourd rattle and rests beside Regina. A young man seated at the rear of the canoe now begins to beat the drum. It is a regular and monotonous drum-beat, deliberately intended to simulate the gallop of a horse and the rhythm of the heart. The shaman and his helpers in the spirit-canoe now visualize the vessel passing down into the earth through 'the crack between the worlds'.

In shamanic belief, man lives on Middle Earth and the two magical domains — the upper and lower universes — are accessible through the trance journey. Often, as experienced shamanic explorers report, the upper and lower worlds tend to merge into a single 'magical reality' which parallels the familiar world. It is here that the shaman must seek a power animal which is willing to offer a new spirit of vitality to Regina.

The sonorous drumming continues, intensifying its rhythm. Harner, meanwhile, has succeeded in locating a spirit in the lower world and clutches it symbolically to his chest. He now rises to his knees still clasping the 'creature' in his hands. The drumming stops as he motions to Regina to sit up. Cupping his hands together above her head, Harner now 'blows' the spirit into her body. He repeats the same action over her chest, whispering to her, 'I have given you a deer', and Regina knows that she must acknowledge this gift in the ceremonial context.

She is a Yoruba black woman, well versed in ritual dance, and she is familiar with the concept of propitiating the healing spirits. Gracefully, ever gracefully, she dances around inside the spirit-canoe, welcoming the presence of her magical creature who has restored health and vitality to her body. With lilting gestures and a lyrical expression of form, she dances her power animal, a dance which is totally unstructured and expresses her inner feelings as they well up within her. Then the work is done. Regina sits down to rest, and Michael Harner announces to the group that the shamanic session is complete. Later Regina tells us how it felt to receive this gift of healing:

'Well, Michael is a very strong shaman,' she says, 'and when he gave me my power animal I felt a surge of energy. The dancing is very spontaneous... I was letting go with all the energy he had breathed in.'

Other members of the group have made their own spirit journeys also — to other regions of the magical terrain. Some of these experiences reveal the extraordinary range of mythological images which become available through the shamanic process. One woman, for example, had ventured to the upper world:

'I was flying. I went up into black sky — there were so many stars — and then I went into an area that was like a whirlwind. I could still see the stars, and I was turning a lot, and my power animals were with me. Then I came up through a layer of clouds and met my teacher — who was a woman I'd seen before. She was dressed in a long, long gown and I wanted to ask her how I could continue with my shamanic work, how to make it more a part of my daily life. Then she took me up through her vagina, actually took me into her, into her belly. I could feel her get pregnant with me and felt her belly stretching. I felt myself inside her. I also felt her put her hands on top of her belly and how large it was! She told me that I should stop breathing, that I should take nourishment from her, and I could actually feel myself stop breathing. I felt a lot of warmth in my belly, as if it were coming into me, and then she stretched further and actually broke apart. Her belly broke apart and I came out of her, and I took it to mean that I needed to use less will in my work, and that I needed to trust her more and let that enter into my daily life. That was the end of my journey — the drum stopped and I came back at that point.'

Michael Harner believes that mythic experiences of this sort are common during the shamanic journey and reveal a dimension of consciousness rarely accessed in daily life:

'Simply by using the technique of drumming, people from time immemorial have been able to pass into these realms which are normally reserved for those approaching death, or for saints. These are the realms of the upper and lower world where one can get information to puzzling questions. This is the Dreamtime of the Australian Aboriginal, the "mythic time" of the shaman. In this area, a person can obtain knowledge that rarely comes to other people.'

This of course begs the question of whether the shaman's journey is just imagination? Is the mythic experience *really* real? Harner's reply is persuasive:

'Imagination is a modern western concept that is outside the realm of shamanism. "Imagination" already prejudges what is happening. I don't think it is imagination as we ordinarily understand it. I think we are entering something which, surprisingly, is universal — regardless of culture. Certainly people are influenced by their own history, their cultural and individual history. But we are beginning to discover a map of the upper and lower world, regardless of culture. For the shaman, what one sees — that's *real*. What one reads out of a book is secondhand information. But just like the scientist, the shaman depends upon first-hand observation to decide what's real. If you can't trust what you see yourself, then what can you trust?'

Harner is now deeply committed to shamanic research, and his workshops at Esalen, in New York, and in Germany and

Austria, have become increasingly popular. In the summer of 1984 he spoke on shamanism at the Academy of Sciences of the USSR in Moscow, attracting the largest audience for a foreign visitor in four years. But the work hasn't stopped there. He is now engaged also in training native tribal peoples in shamanic techniques which have disappeared from their own indigenous cultures. Several groups, including the Sami (formerly known as Lapps) and the Inuit (formerly known as Eskimo) have approached him to help them restore sacred knowledge lost as a result of missionary activity and European colonization. Harner has been able to help them with what he calls 'core shamanism' — general methods consistent with those once used by their ancestors. In this way, he says, 'members of these tribal societies can elaborate and integrate the practices on their own terms in the context of their traditional cultures.'

Activities of a somewhat parallel nature are also taking place at the Ojai Foundation in southern California. Joan Halifax, who is a director of the Foundation, is also an anthropologist and a leading figure in the Human Potential movement. Formerly married to Stanislav Grof, she worked with him treating cancer patients and exploring the similarity between psychedelic states of consciousness and the near-death experience. However, like Harner, her favoured field of inquiry is shamanism and comparative religion. She similarly feels a profound respect for the sacred values of tribal peoples.

The Ojai Valley is beautiful and serene, resplendent with eucalypts, walnut groves, citrus and avocado plantations and the lovely Lake Casitas. It presents a marked contrast to the frenzied clamour of Los Angeles, some two hours' drive to the south.

The first people to occupy the region around Ojai were known as the Oak Grove People (10,000 years BCE). They harvested seeds, nuts and roots, and were in turn replaced by the Chumash Indians, who grew cereals too but also hunted and fished extensively. The name 'Ojai' itself means 'path of the spirit wind', and the valley was revered by the Chumash as a place where war should never be waged. Indeed, the township has now become something of a meditative retreat for several different spiritual groups. Followers of the English mystic, Alice Bailey, have established Meditation Mount near here, and the legendary Indian teacher Jiddu Krishnamurti also has one of his centres nearby. The Ojai Foundation itself lies a little way outside the town at Setukim in the upper Ojai Valley — a region called 'The Place of the Mountain Lion' by the Chumash. The land was earlier the site of the Happy Valley Foundation and had been acquired by Theosophical leader Dr Annie Besant for the purpose of establishing a 'non-sectarian, self-sustaining and environmentally concerned community'.

The Ojai Foundation is not Theosophical but is, nevertheless, true to the spirit of Dr Besant's intent. Here, says Joan Halifax, spokespeople for different spiritual traditions can come to share their learning and their wisdom. There is no attempt to convert. Instead, the Ojai Foundation engenders a respect for different mystical and religious paths, each of which is seen as heading towards the goal of spiritual self-realization.

Many people from different cultures have come to share their knowledge. From the Native American Indian tradition — Brooke Medicine Eagle, a descendant of the Nez Perce holy man Chief Joseph; the Lakota Sioux, Wallace Black Elk, and Harley Swiftdeer, a medicine man who is half Cherokee and half-Irish. Other visitors to the Foundation have included the Tibetan lama Chakdud Tulku Rinpoche; the Australian Aboriginal leader Guboo Ted Thomas; Sufi teacher Pir Vilayat Khan; and Tai Chi master Chungliang Al Huang — among many others. There are some 20 permanent residents at Ojai, most of them living in teepees or yurts, and the formerly barren mountain-top land now yields a rich crop of fruit and vegetables.

'Everything here is cosmic,' says John Gerard, a gardener at Ojai who draws special significance from tending the manure heap, 'and you can always feel the spiritual presence.'

Joan Halifax agrees. For her, the Native American Indian tradition is especially pertinent, for it reveres the earth as sacred. And, as with the goddess-worshippers and wiccans who have tapped the feminine in comparable ways, there is a strong return to the Great Mother:

'In the sacred Sun Dance teachings of the native American people there are two laws, and the first law is that all things are born of woman. So, as we sit here, the clothes that we are wearing, the shoes that we are wearing and the furniture that we're sitting in, the television that we're watching, the cars that we drive in, the houses that we're living in, even the atom bomb — everything came from this earth. And what the Native American people do, in fact indigenous people across this earth do, is recognize the very simple but forgotten fact that everything of substance is born of this earth, that every sentient being is born of a female.

'Indigenous peoples celebrate that knowledge and that wisdom ceremonially, constantly honouring and cherishing the maternal aspect of life — the earth, the feminine, the goddess, the great space in which all is contained. And it's been one of the great sadnesses that I personally feel — as an anthropologist who has worked with people, earth people, all over the planet — that human beings have been sorely and painfully separated from the ground of their health, the ground of their being. Part of what we're trying to do at the Ojai Foundation is to come back into a sacred marriage, if you will, or a sacred way of being, with the earth — recognizing that she is the source of our life, that all things come from her, and that we will all return to her.'

Joan came to Ojai in 1979 from Greenwich Village, New York. She had been a city person, an anthropology tutor at Columbia University, and had worked with Joseph Campbell on an international atlas of mythologies. Life had certainly been interesting before her move to the west coast, but she knew Ojai offered something extra that had been missing in her urban existence:

'At the Foundation we've got the opportunity to open our arms and our homes and the earth in a very special way to people who have only known the city, who have never heard the crickets in summer, who have never seen the kites, the hawks, dancing in the wind...'

At the Ojai centre there are reminders from many cultures that the visitor is on international ground. Tibetan wind chimes dance in the breeze, canvas yurts and teepees stand silhouetted against the distant mountain horizon, and a russet-coloured statue of Lord Buddha has been erected near the sprawling sage bushes.

Beneath a silver birch that stands nearby, a Native American Indian earth circle has been marked on the ground with stones and rocks, and it is here that the sacred pipe is smoked and healing ceremonies performed.

The circle has been divided into the four worlds of Grandmother Earth — with the figure of the coyote allocated to the east, the frog to the south, the rattlesnake to the west and a crystal to the north. For Joan, the coyote, though a trickster, brings insight and illumination; the frog is a creature who dwells beside the 'river of life'; the rattlesnake is a symbol of wisdom, performing the dance of life and death; and the crystal represents absolute truth. In her rituals Joan uses an eagle feather to banish the negative spirits, and she smokes sage in her pipe — a sacred herb taken, with honour, from the land itself.

Some distance away in the hills, the Foundation residents also have their sweat-lodge — once again in accordance with a lifestyle attuned to the Great Mother:

'The sweat-lodge is a method of purification, a method of return to the womb of the Earth Mother. We see the lodge as literally womb-like; the floor is bare earth and the darkness inside the lodge is like being in the belly of the Mother. The rocks have been heated in the fire and brought to the centre of the lodge, and they in turn give their heat to those who are in there praying — praying as they purify themselves that they might become a worthwhile vehicle for the Great Spirit, and live a life of harmony and balance. So when we go into the sweat-lodge we go naked as children, naked as a baby is born into this world. With our hearts open, we ask for help from the Great Spirit — the lodge is a way that we can return to our Mother and ask for guidance from the higher powers.'

For Joan, and other members of the Foundation, the time has now come to bring the sacred mysteries out into the open. She expresses a view that would be shared by many wiccans, neopagans and occultists around the world, that: 'the veil is being lifted off many of the traditions that have kept the teachings a secret.'

It is now late afternoon and a golden haze descends on Ojai.

Muted beams of sunlight reflect from the metallic wind-chimes and shadows lengthen across the earth circle.

'Every one of the teachers who comes here,' says Joan thoughtfully, 'has something in common, and that is a sense of basic goodness. There is a recognition that we all have the same destiny on this planet. There is a great diversity among our beliefs and a great diversity in the different traditions, but we are a common humanity.'

She looks out across the Ojai Valley, a wise woman surveying the terrain. Here, without question, the Earth Mother is honoured and her children have come home.

1. See S. Grof (ed.), *Ancient Wisdom and Modern Science*, 1984, p.25.

2. Maslow's article, 'A Theory of Metamotivation', is included in R. Walsh and F. Vaughan, *Beyond Ego*, Los Angeles 1980.

3. S. Grof, *LSD Psychotherapy*, 1980, p.11.

4. S. Grof, *Realms of the Human Unconscious*, 1976, p.32.

5. S. Grof, *Realms of the Human Unconscious*, p.98.

6. When a person is '*dis*-spirited', their animating force or spirit has departed. The shaman's role is to retrieve it.

People, Organizations, Bookshops and Publications
(cited in book and others)

When writing to any of these organizations please include return postage.

USA

Selena Fox and Jim Alan
Circle, PO Box 219
Mt Horeb, Wisconsin 53572;
Circle Network News

Z Budapest
PO Box 11363
Oakland, California 94611

Starhawk and Luisah Teish
PO Box 14404
San Francisco, California 94114

Dr Gordon Melton
Institute for the Study of American
Religion
University of California/Santa
Barbara
Santa Barbara, California 93106

Dr Michael Aquino and Lilith
Sinclair
The Temple of Set

PO Box 29271
San Francisco, California 94129
Runes

Michael Bertiaux
PO Box 1554
Chicago, Illinois 60690

Dr Michael Harner
Center for Shamanic Studies
PO Box 673, Belden Station
Norwalk, Connecticut 06852
Center Newsletter

Dr Charles Tart
PO Box 371
El Cerrito, California 94530–0371
The Open Mind

Dr Joan Halifax
The Ojai Foundation
PO Box 1620
Ojai, California 93023

Others

Pagana
PO Box 9494
San Jose, California 95157
(Editor: Valerie Voigt)

Magickal Childe Bookshop
35 West 19th Street
New York, NY 1011–4256
(Manager: Herman Slater)

UK and Ireland

Olivia and Lawrence Durdin-
Robertson
The Fellowship of Isis
Clonegal Castle, c/- PO Ennis-
corthy, Ireland
Isian News

Janet and Stewart Farrar
c/- Robert Hale, publishers
45 Clerkenwell Green
London EC1R 0HT, England

The Alchemist's Head Bookshop
10 East Essex Street
Dublin 2, Ireland

Others

Quest
BCM–SCL QUEST
London WC1N 3XX
(Editor: Marian Green)

Aquarian Arrow
BCM–OPAL, London WC1N 3XX
(Editor: Zachary Cox)

The Kabbalist
Metatron Publications
25 Circle Gardens
Merton Park, London SW19 3 JX

The Cauldron
4 Llysonnen Cottages
Llysonnen Road, Meidrim,
Carmarthen
Dyfed, Wales SA35 5ED
(Editor: Mike Howard)

Pagans Against Nukes
Blaenberem
Mynyddcerrig
Llanelli
Dyfed,
Cymru SA15 5BL

Round Merlin's Table
PO Box 215, St Helier, Jersey,
Channel Islands
(Editor: Dolores Ashcroft-
Nowicki)

Ancient Ways
c/- The Alchemist's Head
10 East Essex Street
Dublin 2, Ireland

Australia

Temple of the Mother
GPO Box C118
Perth
Western Australia 6001

Coven of Lothlorien
20 Nurstead Avenue
Bassendean
Perth
Western Australia 6154

People, Organizations, Bookshops and Publications

Walter Glover
11/2 Forest Knoll Avenue
Bondi Beach, NSW 2026
The Art of Rosaleen Norton

Others

Shadowplay
PO Box 343
Petersham, NSW 2049
(Editor: Rhea; Assistant Editor:
Bill Beattie)

Kindred Spirits Quarterly
PO Box 101
Bega, NSW 2550
Edited by a collective

The Source
PO Box 367
Lane Cove, NSW 2066
(Editors: Les and Irena Clinch)

The Australian Shamanic Centre
PO Box 193
Lidcombe, NSW 2141
(Robert Ledwidge)

The Mystical Bookshop
9 Midcity Arcade, 200 Bourke
Street
Melbourne, Victoria 3000
(Manager: Michael Benham)

Mr Thrifty's Bookshop
Shop 7, Martin Place Shopping
Circle
Sydney, NSW 2000
(Manager: Laurie Harris)

The Organizer
Archives Project & the Aquarius
Network
PO Box 570, Parkes, NSW 2870

Bibliography

Adamedes, M., and Paulusz, A., 'Rebirthing', in N. Drury (ed.), *The Bodywork Book*, Prism Press, Dorchester, 1984.

Adler, M., *Drawing Down the Moon*, Beacon Press, Boston, 1981.

Anderson, W. T., *The Upstart Spring: Esalen and the American Awakening*, Addison-Wesley, Reading, Massachusetts, 1983.

Aquino, M., *The Church of Satan*, Temple of Set, San Francisco, 1983.

———, *The Crystal Tablet*, Temple of Set, San Francisco, 1983.

Barker, C. E., *The Churches' Neurosis and Twentieth Century Revelations*, Rider, London, 1975.

Bracelin, J. L., *Gerald Gardner: Witch*, Octagon Press, London, 1960.

Budapest, Z., *The Holy Book of Women's Mysteries*, Parts One and Two, Susan B. Anthony #1 Coven, Los Angeles, 1979–80.

Colquhoun, I., *Sword of Wisdom*, Spearman, London, 1975.

Crowley, A., *Magick in Theory and Practice*, Paris 1929, privately printed (republished by Dover and Castle Books, New York).

———, *The Book of Lies*, London 1913, privately printed (republished by Haydn Press, Ilfracombe, Devon, 1962).

———, *Book Four*, Sangreal Foundation, Dallas 1972.

Crowther, P., *Lid off the Cauldron*, Muller, London, 1981.

Drury, N., *The Path of the Chameleon*, Spearman, London, 1973.

———, *Don Juan, Mescalito and Modern Magic*, Routledge & Kegan Paul, London, 1978 (reprinted 1985).

The Occult Experience

————, *Inner Visions*, Routledge & Kegan Paul, London, 1979.

————, *The Healing Power*, Muller, London, 1981.

————, *The Shaman and the Magician*, Routledge & Kegan Paul, London, 1982.

————, *Vision-Quest*, Prism Press, Dorchester, 1984.

————, *Dictionary of Mysticism and the Occult*, Harper & Row, San Francisco, 1985.

Drury, N., and Tillett, G., *Other Temples, Other Gods*, Methuen, Sydney, 1980 (republished by Hodder & Stoughton, 1982).

Eliade, M., *Occultism, Witchcraft and Cultural Fashions*, University of Chicago Press, Chicago, 1976.

Farrar, J., and S., *Eight Sabbats for Witches*, Hale, London, 1981.

————, *The Witches' Way*, Hale, London, 1984.

————, *The Witches' Bible*, Magickal Childe, New York, 1985.

————, *The Witches' Goddess*, Hale, London, 1987.

Farrar, S., *What Witches Do*, Phoenix, Custer, Washington, 1983.

Fuller, J. O., *The Magical Dilemma of Victor Neuburg*, W. H. Allen, London, 1965.

Gardner, G., *Witchcraft Today*, Rider, London, 1954.

————, *High Magic's Aid*, Michael Houghton, London, 1949 (republished by Weiser, New York).

————, *The Meaning of Witchcraft*, Aquarian Press, London, 1959.

Giger, H. R., *Necronomicon*, Big O Publishing, London, 1978.

————, *N.Y. City*, Ugly Publishing, Zurich, 1981.

————, *Retrospektive 1964–1984*, ABC Verlag, Zurich, 1984.

Grant, K., *Cults of the Shadow*, Muller, London, 1975.

Grof, S., *Realms of the Human Unconscious*, Dutton, New York, 1976.

————, *LSD Psychotherapy*, Hunter House, Pomona, California, 1980.

————, *Ancient Wisdom, Modern Science*, State University of New York Press, Albany, New York, 1984.

Bibliography

Halevi, Z. S., *Adam and the Kabbalistic Tree*, Rider, London, 1974.

——, *Kabbalah: Tradition of Hidden Knowledge*, Thames & Hudson, London, 1975.

Halifax, J., *Shamanic Voices*, Dutton, New York, 1979.

——, *Shaman the Wounded Healer*, Thames & Hudson, London, 1982.

Harner, M., *Hallucinogens and Shamanism*, Oxford University Press, New York, 1973.

——, *The Way of the Shaman*, Harper & Row, San Francisco, 1980.

——, *The Jivaro*, University of California Press, Berkeley, 1984.

Johns, J., *King of the Witches: the World of Alex Sanders*, Coward-McCann, New York, 1969.

King, F., *Ritual Magic in England*, Spearman, London, 1970.

——, *Sexuality, Magic and Perversion*, New English Library, London, 1972.

King, F., and Sutherland, I., *The Rebirth of Magic*. Corgi, London, 1982.

La'Vey, A., *The Satanic Bible*, Avon, New York, 1969.

——, *The Satanic Rituals*, Avon, New York, 1972.

Lesh, C., 'Goddess Worship, the Subversive Religion' in *Twelve Together*, Los Angeles, May 1975.

Lubicz, R. A. S. de, *Her-Bak*, Inner Traditions, New York, 1975.

Lyons, A., *The Second Coming: Satanism in America*, Dodd-Mead, New York, 1970.

Maslow, A., 'A Theory of Metamotivation' in R. N. Walsh and F. Vaughan, *Beyond Ego*, Tarcher, Los Angeles, 1980.

Melton, J. G., *The Encyclopedia of American Religions*, McGrath Publishing, Wilmington, North Carolina, 1978.

Neumann, E., *The Great Mother*, Routledge & Kegan Paul, London, 1954.

Nichols, A., *The Occult: Report of an Anglican Commission of Enquiry*, AIO Publishing, Sydney, 1975.

Norton, R., *The Art of Rosaleen Norton*, second edition, Walter Glover, Sydney, 1982.

————, *Supplement to the Art of Rosaleen Norton*, Walter Glover, Sydney, 1984.

Oesterreich, T. K., *Possession: Demoniacal and Other*, University Books, New York, 1966.

Orr, L., *Rebirthing in the New Age*, Celestial Arts, Millbrae, California, 1980.

Pagels, E., *The Gnostic Gospels*, Weidenfeld & Nicolson, London, 1979.

Roberts, S., *The Magician of the Golden Dawn: the Story of Aleister Crowley*, Contemporary Books, Chicago, 1978.

Robertson, L. D., *God the Mother*, Cesara, Clonegal, 1984.

————, *The Religion of the Goddess*, Cesara, Clonegal, 1984.

————, *The Goddesses of Chaldea, Syria and Egypt*, Cesara, Clonegal, 1975.

————, *The Goddesses of India, Tibet, China and Japan*, Cesara, Clonegal, 1976.

Robertson, O., *Dea: Rites and Mysteries of the Goddess*, Cesara, Clonegal, n.d.

————, *Urania: Ceremonial Magic of the Goddess*, Cesara, Clonegal, n.d.

————, *The Call of Isis*, Cesara, Clonegal, 1975.

————, *Rite of Rebirth*, Cesara, Clonegal, 1977.

————, *Ordination of Priestesses and Priests*, Cesara, Clonegal, 1983.

Russell, J. B., *Satan: the Early Christian Tradition*, Cornell University Press, Ithaca, New York, 1981.

Seligmann, K., *Magic, Supernaturalism and Religion*, Pantheon, New York, 1971.

Starhawk, *The Spiral Dance*, Harper & Row, San Francisco, 1979.

————, *Dreaming the Dark*, Beacon Press, Boston, 1982.

Sutich, A., *The Founding of Humanistic and Transpersonal Psychology — a personal account*, unpublished PhD dissertation presented to the Humanistic Psychology Institute.

Symonds, J., *The Great Beast*, Mayflower, London, 1973.

Bibliography

Tart, C., *Altered States of Consciousness*, Wiley, New York, 1969, (republished by Doubleday).

——, *Transpersonal Psychologies*, Harper & Row, New York, 1975.

Valiente, D., *An ABC of Witchcraft, Past and Present*, Hale, London, 1973.

——, *Witchcraft for Tomorrow*, Hale, London, 1978.

Vaughan, F., 'The Transpersonal Perspective', S. Grof (ed.), *Ancient Wisdom and Modern Science*, State University of New York Press, Albany, New York, 1984.

Walker, B., *Gnosticism: its History and Influence*, Aquarian Press, Wellingborough, Northants, 1983.

Walsh, R. N., and Vaughan, F., *Beyond Ego*, Tarcher, Los Angeles, 1980.